Europe's Unfinished Currency

Europe's Unfinished Currency

The Political Economics of the Euro

Thomas Mayer

ANTHEM PRESS
LONDON · NEW YORK · DELHI

Anthem Press
An imprint of Wimbledon Publishing Company
www.anthempress.com

This edition first published in UK and USA 2012
by ANTHEM PRESS
75-76 Blackfriars Road, London SE1 8HA, UK
or PO Box 9779, London SW19 7ZG, UK
and
244 Madison Ave. #116, New York, NY 10016, USA

British Library Cataloguing-in-Publication Data
A catalogue record for this book is available from the British Library.

Library of Congress Cataloging-in-Publication Data
Mayer, Thomas, 1954-
Europe's unfinished currency : the political economics of the euro /
Thomas Mayer.
p. cm.
Includes index.
ISBN 978-0-85728-548-5 (hbk. : alk. paper)
1. Euro. 2. Currency–European Union countries. 3. Euro area. I. Title.
HG925.M3787 2012
332.4'94–dc23
2012028882

ISBN-13: 978 0 85728 548 5 (Hbk)
ISBN-10: 0 85728 548 3 (Hbk)

This title is also available as an eBook.

Contents

List of Charts, Tables and Textboxes

Charts

Tables

Textboxes

Introduction

'L'Europe se fera par la monnaie ou ne se fera pas.'

—Jacques Rueff,
French post–World War II politician and
economic expert, in 1949[1]

Modern money is a highly political medium. State central banks have the right to create it out of nothing and the monopoly to issue it as legal tender, forcing every creditor to accept it for the settlement of a liability of the debtor. Money is also a political symbol. Coins and banknotes tend to show the faces of presidents, queens, kings or other eminent people, or things conveying a message of political unity. The citizens of post–World War II West Germany drew more national pride from the German mark (D-Mark) than from anything else. When the Berlin Wall fell, their East German fellow citizens shouted in the streets: 'Wenn die D-Mark nicht zu uns kommt, dann kommen wir zu ihr!'[2] Hence, it would be a mistake to look for the roots of the euro in the economic rather than the political domain. In this book I tell the story of the euro as a hugely ambitious political project pursued with an occasionally reckless negligence of economics.

Without this recklessness the euro may never have come into existence. Because of it, the euro experienced a deep crisis after a fairly happy childhood. Future historians will look at this crisis either as the catharsis needed to mature the young European currency or as the moment when the unstoppable force of political ambition met the immovable object of economic reality. Ever since I began to work on European monetary integration as a young economist at the International Monetary Fund (IMF), I have struggled to reconcile the politics with the economics of the undertaking. My European heart has been beating for the economic and monetary union of Europe; my economist head has continuously taken issue with the project. So, where do I come out at the end of this book? Fellow economists will have guessed the answer: with a conditional positive prognosis. Yes, I believe the euro can work, but only if we repair its faulty original architecture in the right way. A new framework for the euro must be based on two elementary principles: first, the euro must be a nonpolitical currency, shielded from any form of fiscal dominance by EMU member states; second, sovereignty and liability in essential fiscal policy matters must be firmly aligned at the national level.

My story begins in Chapter 1 with the origins of the euro in the quest for the unification of Europe. This has been a project of historic proportions propelled by the lessons from the most atrocious period of war in the history of mankind, which began with the murder of the heir to the Austro-Hungarian throne in Sarajevo on 28 June 1914 and ended with the downfall of Nazi Germany and surrender of the German armed forces on 8 May 1945. In between the wars of 1914–18 and 1939–45 was a period resembling more an armistice than peace, poisoned by the Treaty of Versailles, which bred resentment and revanchism.

Towards the end of World War II, enlightened politicians of the allied powers against Germany – most notably within the French government in exile – were determined not to repeat the mistakes made in the Treaty of Versailles and decided to bind Germany into a European structure after its defeat. Thus, the European Coal and Steel Community (ECSC) was founded to start the process of European unification with the goal to ensure everlasting peace in Europe by securing European nations in an ever-closer net of integration.

Chapter 2 shows how the process of Western European integration received an unforeseen twist when the Berlin Wall fell and the Soviet Union collapsed. To ensure a firm anchoring of a newly united Germany in Europe, politicians – especially the French – insisted on the creation of a monetary union. However, the past success in creating a European union in the west and the disappearance of the military threat from the east made war in the centre of Europe unthinkable. As a result, European integration lost its deepest inspiration. The consequence was that the momentum towards a political union of European states faded. Economic and Monetary Union (EMU), which was expected to be fortified by the creation of political union, lost the prospect of eventually reaching a safe harbour. It was launched nonetheless.

The review of past monetary unions in Chapter 3 illustrates that launching EMU and creating the euro without some form of political union was indeed a risky undertaking. No monetary union has so far survived without being eventually bolstered by some form of political union of its member states. Moreover, even when monetary unions were backed by political union, severe frictions over fiscal policy often continued until the central authority had become the dominating fiscal and political power.

Against this historical background, the architecture of EMU seemed rather fragile and hardly a durable construct to house a common currency for Europe.

Nevertheless, as discussed in Chapter 4, the euro enjoyed a fairly happy childhood. During the first ten years of its existence, most countries, with the exception of Germany and Italy, experienced fairly healthy growth. Countries such as Ireland, Greece and Spain seemed to catch up with the larger countries in Central Europe. The European Central Bank (ECB) kept inflation at its target and the euro became the second most important international reserve currency after the US dollar. To be fair, there were continuous battles over fiscal policy with few countries observing the fiscal discipline they had committed themselves to in the Stability and Growth Pact. But these skirmishes appeared to matter little. Rising current account imbalances among EMU member countries were interpreted as a sign of financial market integration, with financial capital flowing unhindered by exchange rate risk to countries offering the highest return.

With the escalation of the financial crisis from a problem in the subprime segment of the US mortgage market in 2007 to a full-blown crisis of government finances culminating in the near-default of Greece in April 2010, the seemingly happy childhood of the euro was found to have been an illusion. As I argue in Chapter 5, while the global credit bubble expanded, cheap credit from the capital markets had papered over the life-threatening cracks in the architecture of EMU. When the bubble burst, the glue that had held the euro together dissolved. Frantic activities by the fiscal and monetary authorities prevented a sudden collapse; but in their effort to save the euro the authorities entered legally unchartered territory as they had to operate outside the agreed treaties. As a result, EMU fell into a crisis of legitimacy. Critics accused governments of having broken the no-bailout rule established in Article 125 of the EU treaty (TFEU) when they gave assistance to Greece and other countries, and they accused the ECB of having flouted Article 123 (which forbids monetary financing of government deficits) when it started to buy government bonds of troubled EMU member states in the secondary market. Bundesbank president Axel Weber and ECB chief economist Jürgen Stark resigned from the Governing Council of the ECB over these bond purchases.

But this was not the only consequence of the disappearance of cheap and ample credit. The euro area also entered a balance-of-payments crisis as external current accounts and internal government budget deficits could no longer be smoothly funded in the markets and scared investors fled countries with worrisome financial fundamentals. Chapter 6 explains how the Eurosystem of central banks stepped in to provide cheap, unconditional and unlimited balance-of-payment credits to needy countries. Policymakers and the general public intensely debated fiscal assistance to countries cut off from the capital markets by the IMF, fellow countries and EU institutions. But they failed to see the much larger balance-of-payment assistance provided by the Eurosystem, which reached a trillion euros by mid-2012.

How can EMU be saved from collapse? Some politicians and observers have argued that countries need to rush forward into fiscal and eventually political union, the 'United States of Europe'. In Chapter 7 I make the case that this is unlikely to happen and would probably not even help, as it is entirely unrealistic to expect such a union to have a politically and fiscally dominating federal government. The historical review of Chapter 3 suggests that this would be needed to ensure fiscal policy discipline through political means. It seems that the only realistic option is to go back to the original design of EMU where each country is responsible for its government finances and the ECB aims for price stability in the union. The historical model that comes closest to the fiscal policy requirements for European EMU is that of the United States in the nineteenth century. States were sovereign in their budget decisions but also fully responsible for their finances and left to default on their debt when they had overborrowed. Pressure for fiscal policy discipline had to come from the market as the political influence of the federal government was limited by its fairly small size.

It is of course one thing to design the future architecture of EMU. It is another to get there. As long as governments remain highly indebted and at risk of being suddenly cut off from market funding, they need a lender of last resort like any other debtor of systemic importance to the financial sector. Therefore, in Chapter 8 I discuss who can act as a lender of last resort. Unfortunately, the debate of this question has been rather confused. Some commentators have assigned this role to the ECB without any qualification; others have categorically rejected this. In my view, however, a crisis management mechanism, such as the European Stability Mechanism (ESM), must have access to central bank credit as a last resort during a financial crisis, when capital markets are shut for virtually all borrowers, including the crisis mechanism itself. Hence, the ESM should have the backing of the ECB, but recourse to ECB credit must be subject to close scrutiny and be allowed only when it promotes rather than undermines price stability. In other words, the ESM needs to be developed into a European Monetary Fund (EMF).

Chapter 9 reviews the political discussion of the euro rescue. It has been widely argued that Germany is the main beneficiary of EMU and hence should bear the brunt of the costs for saving it. I take issue with this view and make the case that the economic benefits of EMU are quite moderate. European monetary unification needs to be justified on political grounds. Unfortunately, the political management of the euro crisis has added to the erosion of the political cohesion of EMU members that began with the fall of the Berlin Wall. Yet, a reversal of this process and a strengthening of political cohesion are essential to prevent the failure and break-up of EMU. Still, hopes to impose fiscal policy discipline on the member states of EMU through intergovernmental treaties are likely to be unrealized. For this to work, EMU would need a politically and fiscally dominating central government, which is not on the cards. Hence, the only available option to enforce fiscal policy discipline is to allow market forces to operate.

What are the political grounds on which the euro can be justified when EMU is no longer needed as a stepping stone to political union and guaranteed peace in Europe? In Chapter 10 I argue that in a world of free capital movements small countries have hardly any policy sovereignty left to protect themselves when large countries or regions experience financial or monetary crises. By pooling national monetary sovereignty in EMU, European countries can retain joint policy sovereignty at the global level. This is all the more important as I see clouds on the horizon for the present US-centric global monetary system.

Chapter 11 discusses a new EMU architecture based on five building blocks: (1) EMU governments must be held fully liable for their financial decisions; (2) the central bank must ensure price stability and provide funds of last resort to all systemically important debtors; (3) the central bank

lends funds of last resort in close cooperation with the
European Systemic Risk Board and an EMF; (4) the EMF
monitors national economic policies, provides adjustment
funding to illiquid governments and conducts orderly debt
restructurings for insolvent governments and banks; (5)
the European System of Financial Supervision ensures
an appropriate financial architecture where public sector
debt is considered subject to default risk, cooperates with
the EMF in restructuring or resolving insolvent banks
and manages a common deposit insurance scheme. Since
not all present and future EMU member countries can
be expected to be or remain fit for EMU, exit from EMU
without exit from the EU should become possible as a
measure of last resort to stabilize the economy.

Without a new architecture along the lines sketched
above, the long-term survival of EMU in its present form
would seem to be at risk. I can envisage two potential
mutations of EMU in the future. In the first, the ECB
would be dragged into monetizing the deficits and debt of
insolvent governments and banks. Over time this would
lead to the formation of a new, hard currency union around
Germany, with the existing EMU continuing as a 'soft
currency' union. The hard union could exist within the soft
union, with cash shared by all members but the new hard
money adopted only by the financially strong members
as a second-tier, entirely virtual currency. Apart from the
AAA-rated countries – Germany, the Netherlands, Finland
and Luxembourg – Austria and a few other central European
EMU member countries with strong government finances
might opt for the hard currency. Given the continuing
use of euro bills and coins, such a union within the union
may just be tolerable politically for France and other Latin
European countries with a preference for a soft currency
policy and a higher tolerance of inflation. In the second

mutation, EMU would be reduced to a hard currency union (in the composition sketched above plus, for political reasons, France) by the exit of all countries unable to operate under a hard budget constraint. These countries would then go back to their national currencies. In view of the economic pain for weak countries of exiting EMU, the first mutation would seem to be more likely than the second.

Chapter 1

A Question of War and Peace

'Europe cannot be made in one stroke, nor can it be made through simple aggregation: it will emerge through concrete facts, which at first will create solidarity of deeds. The unification of European nations requires that the century-old adversity between France and Germany will be eliminated. The work under way in the first place has to affect Germany and France.'

—Robert Shuman,
French foreign minister, 9 May 1950[1]

Already towards the end of World War II, visionary French politicians, such as Jean Monnet and Robert Marjolin, concluded that a defeated Germany would have to be bound into a European structure in order to avoid a repeat of the experience after World War I. At that time, France, led by Prime Minister Georges Clemenceau, had insisted on a peace treaty that was not only to keep Germany powerless but also prevent its economy from recovering from the war for a long time. Mired in nineteenth-century thinking, the victorious European powers had expected that Germany would not only pay for her own reconstruction but also finance their war debt and economic recovery from the destruction experienced in 1914–18. The Inter-Allied Reparations Commission in 1921 initially put the reparations at 269 billion German gold marks or 64 billion US gold standard dollars (equivalent to USD 785 billion in 2011 prices). But soon it became clear that this demand was impossible to fulfil. As Germany had difficulties making the payments, they were reduced to 226 billion gold marks in the Dawes Plan of 1924, and then, as Germany defaulted again, reduced further to 112 billion gold marks under the Young Plan of 1929. The latter envisaged payments over a period of 59 years, with the last instalment due in 1988.

The harsh conditions dictated in the Treaty of Versailles led to deep-seated German resentment and helped pave the way to German revanchism and eventually to Nazi Germany. When Hitler came to power in 1933 and ended all war reparations, Germany had paid only 20 billion gold marks. At the time, very few people recognized the dangers of the harsh treatment of Germany. One of them was John Maynard Keynes, who in June 1919 resigned from the British Treasury in protest over the size of the reparations. In his famous treatise 'The Economic Consequences of the Peace' published in the same year, he wrote:

> Europe, if she is to survive her troubles, will need so much magnanimity from America, that she must herself practise it. It is useless for the Allies, hot from stripping Germany and one another, to turn for help to the United States to put the States of Europe, including Germany, on to their feet again.[2]

Mindful of the developments in the 1920s and 30s, Robert Marjolin, an economic adviser to the exiled de Gaulle government and later head of the Organisation for European Economic Co-operation (the predecessor of the Organisation for Economic Co-operation and Development) and a commissioner of the European Economic Community (EEC), in a memorandum to Jean Monnet in 1944 argued for the construction of a unified Europe. In his memoirs, he recalls: 'A grandiose conception, I wrote, extremely difficult to implement, but representing the only hope of salvation for our western civilization in Europe. The first stage would be to form a federation comprising Britain, France, Benelux, and Germany.'[3] He quotes from his 1944 paper:

> In the economic sphere, the unification of Europe would be marked by a progressive dismantlement of all barriers to the free circulation of goods, persons, and capital, by a rational division of labour among the different regions, by a progressive equalisation of living standards across the continent (though it will never be possible to achieve complete equalization...) The European economy as a whole would receive an extraordinarily powerful impetus from unification of the European market.[4]

Under the leadership of their French colleagues, politicians on the Continent set the stage for the creation of the ECSC, where industries important for the conduct of war were brought under a European umbrella. But European integration was not supposed to end there. Ever-closer economic integration was seen to drive forward political integration. Already in 1950, German chancellor Adenauer

in an interview with International News Service proposed
a political union between Germany and France:

> A union between France and Germany would give
> new life and new impetus to a very sick Europe. It
> would be of great influence both psychologically and
> materially and would unleash forces that surely would
> rescue Europe. I believe this is the only way to achieve
> the unification of Europe.[5]

The goal of political union was pursued by making concrete
steps forward at the economic level, including over time the
move to the EEC, the creation of the European Union and the
Single European Market and eventually the establishment
of EMU (see textbox below for a short history of European
integration).[6] The most fervent advocates of integration
saw the process as a 'chain reaction'. According to Walter
Hallstein, a close collaborator of Adenauer and a president
of the Commission of the EEC from 1958 to 1967, the
'inner logic of integration' would lead from the ECSC to
customs union, a common agricultural and commercial
policy and eventually political union: the United States of
Europe. However, the vision of a European federation was
quite controversial. Against the federalist model popular
in Germany and the smaller European states stood the
concept of Europe as a union of sovereign nation states.
This view was most strongly held in France. As Marjolin
put it:

> Between maintenance of national sovereignties in
> toto and dismantlement of the latter, there is a middle
> way. For me, this middle way represented the reality,
> the hypothetical extremes – full maintenance of
> sovereignties or their dismantlement – being mental

constructs. The middle way was a treaty whereby the signatory states would pledge themselves to one another indefinitely and undertake to carry out certain acts by specified dates, such as the progressive abolition of customs duties and import quotas, the gradual derestriction of movements of labour and capital, the organisation of agricultural markets, and so on. After a transition period, which might vary according to the circumstances, the result would be a Europe which, if perhaps not wholly unified economically, would nevertheless present a degree of unity unachieved hitherto.[7]

The history of economic integration in Europe: Timeline of major events

1951	ECSC → *(1) Preferential Zone*
1957	Treaties of Rome: • EEC → *(2) Free Trade Area* • European Atomic Energy Community (EURATOM) • ECSC
1960	European Free Trade Area (EFTA): founding members were the 'Outer Seven' (Austria, Denmark, Norway, Portugal, Sweden, Switzerland, UK)
(1965) 1967	Merger Treaty: ECSC, EURATOM and EEC merged into European Community (EC) → *(3) Customs Union*
1972	Exchange Rate Mechanism (ERM): European currency snake
1973	Northern enlargement 1: accession of Denmark, UK and Ireland
1979	European Monetary System (EMS), including ECU as a basket currency

(Continued)

1981	Southern enlargement 1: accession of Greece
1985	Southern enlargement 2: accession of Spain and Portugal
1985	Schengen Treaty signed. Schengen area came into existence 10 years later in 1995
(1986) 1987	Single European Act • First major treaty revision since 1957 • Agreement on full removal of all tariff and nontariff barriers in the European Single Market (ESM) until 1992
(1992) 1993	Maastricht Treaty: → *(4) Common Market* Treaty reform – three pillars: • EC (supranational) • Common Foreign and Security Policy (CFSP, intergovernmental) • Justice and Home Affairs (JHA, intergovernmental) Agreement on 3 stages to EMU: 1. 1990: Free capital movement 2. 1994: Convergence of macro policies 3. 1999: Launch of the euro
(1993) 1994	European Economic Area: EFTA plus EU-12 minus Switzerland
1995	Northern enlargement 2: Finland, Sweden, Austria
1996	Broad Economic Policy Guidelines as a means for economic policy coordination → *(5) Economic Union*
1997	Stability and Growth Pact
(1997) 1999	Amsterdam Treaty • More power for European Parliament, strengthening the rights of citizens
1999	Third Stage of EMU: European Central Bank; launch of the euro as accounting unit → *(6) Currency Union*
2002	Euro notes and coins replace national currency

(2001) 2003	Treaty of Nice: amendment of majority rules in the council. Strengthening the principle of qualified majority; weighing population
2004	Eastern enlargement 1: Cyprus, Czech Republic, Estonia, Hungary, Latvia, Lithuania, Malta, Poland, Slovak Republic, Slovenia
2007	Eastern enlargement 2: Romania, Bulgaria
2009	Lisbon Treaty: institutional reforms, more qualified majority voting, closer economic coordination between EMU member states, EU becomes legal personality
2010	Euro Crisis: EMU countries agree on support programmes for Greece (2 May) and other EMU countries (9 May). Founding of EFSM and EFSF
2011	Signing of ESM Treaty
2012	Signing of Fiscal Treaty

The close relationship between France and Germany as the engine for European integration was reflected in the close personal relationship between the political leaders of the two nations. President de Gaulle and Chancellor Adenauer started the tradition that was carried on by, among others, Valéry Giscard d'Estaing and Helmut Schmidt, and François Mitterrand and Helmut Kohl. During most of the post–World War II period, this was not an equal partnership. There was a clear hierarchy: France was in the political lead and Germany followed, often backing the European project with its renewed financial power. But the relationship benefited both partners: Germany was able to influence the international political debate by having France speak for her as well as for herself and France could leverage her political weight via German economic power. The process of European integration was driven forward by the political elites in both countries. The general public retained more or less sceptical attitudes towards the European project and had to be pulled along by its political leaders.

Early on, the creation of a common currency was seen as being of particular importance for European unification. According to the 'inner logic of European integration', currency union would inevitably drive Europe towards political union. Already in 1949, Jacques Rueff, a famous French economist and government adviser, had predicted that 'Europe will be created through its money or not at all'. Money has of course always played an eminently political role. As the anthropologist David Graeber has pointed out, in early societies coins were often issued first to soldiers. Requiring the civilian population to pay their taxes with coins created demand for them. Thus, rulers used money to measure the tax obligations of their subjects and fund a standing army.[8] Rueff's call for monetary integration must also be seen against the background of the disparate conditions of European countries immediately after World War II. Currencies were not convertible and trade was conducted under bilateral agreements, without the possibility of balancing the deficit of one trading partner with the surplus of another. When the bilateral credit lines granted in 1946 and 1947 had been exhausted, the result was a complete jam in the intra-European payment system.[9] This led eventually to the creation of the European Payments Union (EPU) in 1950, which allowed the netting out of all deficits and surpluses of a country vis-à-vis the EPU on a monthly basis. Monthly net positions were cumulated over time and settled periodically. Up to a certain 'quota' (based on trade turnover), countries could settle imbalances with the EPU in credit, but when the imbalance exceeded a certain threshold, payment had to be made in gold. Given the scarcity of countries' gold holdings at the time, debtor countries were hard pressed to adjust when imbalances exceeded the size that could be settled with credit.

In a telling prelude to the developments of 2010–12, when a country accumulated a deficit larger than its quota and lacked the gold to settle it, the EPU gave financial assistance, provided that the country committed itself to pursuing an economic adjustment programme. The first country receiving such assistance was Germany, which in 1950 developed a large current account deficit in excess of its quota. Germany's EPU-funded adjustment programme was successful and the country achieved a current account surplus in 1951, the first of many more in the following years and decades. However, the EPU became redundant and was officially dissolved in 1958, when European countries had accumulated sufficient gold reserves to make their currencies convertible. Only with currency convertibility achieved did the Bretton Woods exchange rate system eventually become fully operational in Europe.

Concern about the implications of a revaluation of the D-Mark and the Dutch guilder in 1961 for support prices in the context of the Common Agricultural Policy (CAP) prompted the EEC Commission to argue for a permanent fixing of EEC exchange rates.[10] In October 1964, Marjolin, in his function as a commissioner, told central bank governors of the EEC to prepare for monetary unification. In 1965, he declared that monetary union was 'an inevitable obligation'.[11] However, his call fell on deaf ears, especially at the Bundesbank and the Dutch central bank, which thought that the preconditions for a monetary union as spelt out in the economic literature in the early 1960s by Robert Mundell and Peter Kenen were far from fulfilled. This episode highlights a dispute over European monetary integration that has been going on virtually ever since the beginning of the process. One camp, dubbed 'monetarists', has argued that monetary integration must drive economic and political integration. Monetarists were in favour of a common currency early on, expecting the conditions for a smooth-functioning EMU to come into place in due course. Present-day monetarists would take the EMU crisis of 2010–12 in their stride, seeing it as a necessary catalyst for the fortification of the currency union and a driver towards further political integration. The other camp, dubbed 'economists', has argued that the economic and fiscal conditions for monetary union must be established first before EMU can begin. Consequently, economists today would interpret the most recent crisis as proof that the necessary conditions of EMU had not been fulfilled at its start. They would in present circumstances probably be more sceptical about the future of EMU than monetarists.

Despite the controversy over EMU in the mid-60s, the first serious attempt at creating a common European currency was made in 1970. The initiative came primarily from German chancellor Willy Brandt and was turned into an action plan by Luxembourg's prime minister Pierre Werner. The so-called 'Werner Plan' envisaged the creation of a monetary union in several stages, to be completed in 1980. Compared to the later Maastricht Treaty, the Werner Plan was relatively short with regard to the creation of the central bank, only recommending a community system of central banks along the lines of the US Federal Reserve System, but it was fairly specific with regard to the need for joint economic policies. Thus, it envisaged a 'centre of decision for economic policy', politically responsible to the European Parliament, exerting decisive influence over countries' economic policies, including fiscal policy:

> The essential features of the whole of the public budgets, and in particular variations in their volume, the size of balances and the methods of financing them or utilising them, will be decided at the Community level; regional and structural policies will no longer be exclusively within the jurisdiction of the member countries; a systematic and continuous consultation between the social partners will be ensured at the Community level.[12]

To avoid regional and structural disequilibria despite increased capital and labour mobility, there would have to be public financial transfers.

In contrast to the Maastricht Treaty, the Werner Plan was more concerned about the long-run risks of divergence in economic policies and developments and saw therefore the need for more Community authority over budget policies and for a joint incomes policy. Its emphasis on economic policy coordination made it more acceptable to sceptical economists and therefore probably contributed to its adoption by European policymakers. However, the weakness of the plan lay in its implicit reliance on the Bretton Woods system of quasi-fixed exchange rates, where the exchange rate to the US dollar played the role of the monetary anchor for non-US central banks. Without this system, the Werner Plan had no answer to how a common monetary policy should be conducted. Hence, it was only logical that the Werner Plan was abandoned when the Bretton Woods system collapsed in 1973 on the back of US balance-of-payments deficits, incurred in part by the monetary funding of military expenses abroad. The latter led to an international excess supply of US dollars that exceeded the demand for dollars as international reserve currency and eventually induced other countries to let their currencies float against the dollar and each other.

But not everything laid down in the Werner Plan was given up. It described in some detail the need for and the mechanics of narrowing the bilateral fluctuation margins of European currencies against each other within the Bretton Woods system in the run-up to EMU. The feature of narrow fluctuation margins of intra-European exchange rates was introduced in 1972 for a range of countries, including France, Germany and, for a short period, even the UK. This arrangement survived the collapse of the Werner Plan. However, during the following years, the so-called 'snake' of European currencies that were linked to each other by narrow exchange rate fluctuation margins in a world of generally floating exchange rates saw numerous exits and entries and exchange rate realignments. Towards the end of the 1970s, the snake had degenerated into an exchange rate system of Germany and a few smaller countries. European heavy weights such as France, Italy and the UK were missing. The end of the 1970s was also a period of diminishing US political and economic weight, prompting European powers to seek greater independence from the US. This, and the desire to bind a politically unstable Italy that flirted with communism more firmly into European structures, induced German chancellor Helmut Schmidt and French president Valéry Giscard d'Estaing to make another push for European monetary integration. Based on a plan developed by the European Commission led by Roy Jenkins, the European Council of Bremen in 1978 decided to create a 'European Monetary System' (EMS) that officially took effect in March 1979.

The EMS was to differ from the snake in one very important respect: it was supposed to be a symmetrical system of bilateral exchange rates. The snake had been dominated by Germany, which pursued a domestically oriented monetary policy and thus provided a monetary anchor for the smaller countries that aimed to stabilize their currencies vis-à-vis the D-Mark. For France and other potential heavyweight members of the EMS, this asymmetry was not acceptable. Members of the snake, on the other hand, wanted to move their arrangement into the new EMS while preserving the nature of their system, which they felt had worked well. As so often in European politics, the difference in views was papered over. The EMS was constructed as a grid of bilateral exchange rates with fluctuation margins of +/– 2.25 per cent around the central rates (with an exception of +/– 6 per cent for Italy), and at the same time as a line of exchange rates of national currencies against a common unit of account, the ECU, which was defined as a basket of the currencies participating in the EMS. However, in view of the technical complexities involved in establishing foreign exchange intervention rules against a currency basket and the established practice in the snake, France conceded that compulsory interventions would only have to be made when two currencies reached their bilateral margins. In return, it was agreed that the divergence of a currency against its ECU central rate would be calculated and expressed in the form of a 'divergence indicator', which took the value of·100 per cent when a currency had reached its maximum allowed divergence from its central rate. When a currency reached 75 per cent, authorities were expected to intervene in the foreign exchange market, take policy measures to adjust the economy and eventually change the central rate of the currency. However, in the later practical operation of the EMS, the efforts at making

the system more 'symmetrical' failed and the central rates
of currencies against the ECU and the divergence indicator
played only a marginal role.[13] To the disappointment of
France, the EMS assumed more the nature of the snake,
with the D-Mark being the anchor currency, than the new
symmetrical arrangement that France had wanted. In an
analysis of developments up to the early 1990s, Gros and
Thygesen found that 'Germany had a strong influence on
the other EMS countries, but there was also some weak
influence the other way round'.[14] The asymmetric nature
of the system, which gave the D-Mark and the Bundesbank
a pivotal role in its operation, was a continuous source
of dissatisfaction for other larger participating countries
within the EMS. It was also an important driver for the
eventual creation of European Economic and Monetary
Union.

The asymmetrical nature of the EMS was never clearer
than in the exchange rate crisis of 1992–3. On 7 February
1992, the European Council concluded the Maastricht
Treaty, which laid the ground for EMU (more on this
below). On 2 June 1992, however, the Danish population
in a referendum narrowly rejected the Maastricht Treaty.
This and mounting economic problems in a number of
European countries (due to a lack of competitiveness and
high interest rates imported from Germany, which was
fighting inflation triggered by unification) led to exchange
rate tensions within the EMS. Market participants
anxiously awaited the result of the French referendum on
the Maastricht Treaty, scheduled for September. There was
general agreement that a 'non' to Maastricht by the French
would put an end to European monetary integration and
perhaps even lead to its unravelling. On 14 September,
the Italian lira succumbed to the pressure in the foreign
exchange market and was devalued by 7 per cent. Only

three days later, on 17 September, the Spanish peseta was devalued by 5 per cent. On the same day, which entered UK history as 'Black Wednesday', the pound sterling left the EMS, followed by the lira. Then, at the referendum in France on 20 September, 51.05 per cent of the voters were in favour and 48.95 per cent against the Maastricht Treaty and the creation of EMU. The razor-thin majority for EMU in the country most fervently pushing for a common currency convinced financial markets that the project was in deep trouble. As a result, market participants built up large short positions in the French franc against the D-Mark. It seemed inevitable that the franc would share the fate of the other European currencies and be devalued against the D-Mark or even expelled from the EMS. The 'battle of the franc' began.

During the week following the 20 September referendum there were fierce debates between French and German officials on how to resist market pressure for franc devaluation. The French wanted a joint declaration in support of the D-Mark–franc parity and an unlimited credit line from the Bundesbank to defend the franc. The Germans, led by the Bundesbank, resisted. Helmut Schlesinger, then president of the Bundesbank, is said to have told a gathering of high-level French and German officials: 'I will not sign any joint declaration by the French and German central banks on maintaining the parity. Don't count on me for that.'[15] However, Chancellor Kohl leaned heavily on the Bundesbank and eventually persuaded it to raise the credit line for the Banque de France to DM 39 billion. Moreover, on 23 September the French and German central banks and finance ministries published a joint communiqué expressing their determination to hold the parity. Behind the scenes the Bundesbank sent signals to financial market participants that speculation against the French franc would be unsuccessful. George Soros, the famous hedge fund manager credited with forcing sterling to leave the EMS, later recalled: 'I felt safe betting with the Bundesbank. The Bundesbank clearly wanted the pound and lira devalued, but it was prepared to defend the French franc. I did better than some others by sticking to the Bundesbank's side.'[16]

With this large-scale intervention, as well as interest rate increases in France and cuts in Germany, the speculation against the franc was quelled, at least for the moment. In a speech before the German parliament on 25 September, Chancellor Kohl declared:

> [European unification] gave us Germans the chance for the reunification of our fatherland, because it created the very trust in a democratic Germany, which was the precondition for the agreement of our neighbours, partners, and friends to German unity... For the exchange rate between the French franc and the D-Mark there is no need for adjustment, as both governments and central banks jointly found, because France has achieved important successes for stability. Price and cost conditions are today there more favourable than here.[17]

However, the reprieve was only temporary. Tensions in the EMS continued, forcing further devaluations of the Spanish peseta and the Portuguese escudo. Most worryingly, the French franc remained under severe pressure against the background of a weakening French economy. Finally, to preserve the EMS at least on paper, the European Monetary Committee (the body in charge of dealing with exchange rate issues) on 2 August 1993 decided to widen the fluctuation bands to +/− 15 per cent.

In practice, this meant that the European currencies would float against each other from then on. The French central bank governor de Larosière later recalled:

> The initial French proposal was to ask the Germans to leave the EMS, on the grounds that it was German policy that was creating strains in the system. One of the first to speak on this idea were the Dutch, who immediately indicated that they would follow the D-Mark. So did the Belgians. I then telephoned [French finance minister] Balladur to say that the idea would not work. I realized that the system would only survive with a very large widening of bands.[18]

It seems quite likely that any attempt for Germany to leave the euro today would trigger a similar reaction by a number of euro area countries sharing Germany's preference for low inflation and a hard currency.

Chapter 2

No Longer a Question of War and Peace

'Let us now talk about the German atom bomb.'
'You know we don't have the atomic bomb—what do you mean?'
'I mean the D-Mark.'

—Jacques Attali, French presidential advisor, in a discussion with German officials in 1987[1]

The end of the Cold War and fall of the Berlin Wall in 1989 was not only a watershed event for the world. It also fundamentally changed the nature of European integration. On the one hand, the prospect of re-unifying Germany opened the door for the country to give up its beloved D-Mark – a symbol of its post–World War II economic and political achievements – in exchange for a common European currency. Firmer integration of Germany in the EU was the price President Mitterrand demanded from Chancellor Kohl for France's backing of German unification. Without French backing, unification would have re-opened long-buried political divisions in Europe. On the other hand, it fundamentally changed Germany's relationship to France and its other European partners. The united, fully sovereign Germany was no longer willing to remain in the political shadow of France and to treat its own national interests as subservient to those of the Union.

The asymmetric nature of the EMS had vexed Germany's partners for some time. Following the exchange rate realignment of January 1987, when the French franc, the Italian lira and the Danish krone were devalued by 3 per cent against the D-Mark, and the Belgian/Luxembourg franc by 2 per cent, French finance minister Balladur sent a memorandum to his colleagues in the Council of Finance Ministers (ECOFIN), in which he indirectly complained about the inherent bias of the EMS in favour of Germany:

> Ultimately it is the central bank whose currency is at the lower end of the permitted range which has to bear the cost. However, it is not necessarily the currency at the lower end of the range which is the source of the tension. The discipline imposed by the exchange rate mechanism may, for its part, have good effects when it serves to put a constraint on economic and monetary policies which are insufficiently rigorous. It produces an abnormal situation when its effect is to exempt any countries whose policies are too restrictive from the necessary adjustment. Thus, the fact that some countries have piled up current account surpluses for several years equal to between 2 and 3 percent of their GDPs constitutes a grave anomaly. This asymmetry is one of the reasons for the present tendency of European currencies to rise against the dollar and the currencies tied to it. This rise is contrary to the fundamental interest of Europe and of its constituent economies. We must therefore find a new system under which this problem cannot arise.[2]

Balladur's memorandum was echoed only one month later by a similar epistle from Italy's finance minister Giuliano Amato. He complained that the role of Germany in the EMS was such that it 'removed growth potential from other nations'. In these circumstances, the already decided reduction of exchange controls and the prospective complete liberalization of capital controls were risky for Italy. Therefore, Amato proposed 'a recycling mechanism which could borrow funds on the market and reallocate them in such a way as to compensate the inflow and outflow of capital'.[3] Although they did not explicitly spell out the implications of their criticism, both finance ministers seemed to suggest that further steps towards European monetary integration were required to remedy the deficiencies they had identified within the EMS. This is at least how the German side interpreted the interventions.

In a surprising move, Germany's foreign minister Hans-Dietrich Genscher in 1988 issued a memorandum entitled 'A European currency area and a European central bank', in which he called for monetary union to complete the European Internal Market. In the tradition of the monetarists, he saw a common currency and a central bank as the catalysts to achieve the convergence of economic policies necessary to make EMU work. Genscher proposed the creation of an expert group that was supposed to develop within a year concrete proposals for the creation of EMU.

Germany's finance minister Gerhard Stoltenberg was taken aback by Genscher's initiative and a few weeks later followed up with a memorandum of his own. In the spirit of the economists, Stoltenberg took a much more cautious view, emphasizing the need for economic convergence as a prerequisite for monetary union and the need for backing it up with further political integration. The Bundesbank, and especially its president Karl-Otto Pöhl, took a similarly critical view. Nevertheless, at their summit in Hannover on June 27–8, European leaders under the chairmanship of Chancellor Kohl decided to set up a group of experts to develop a roadmap towards EMU. Only a few months later in April 1989, the committee, headed by the president of the European Commission Jacques Delors, presented the results of its deliberations. It recommended a three-stage process towards EMU.[4]

The steps towards EMU were supposed to be 'discrete but evolutionary' and be accompanied by closer monetary and economic integration. The committee set only the starting date for the first stage at 1 July 1990, but left the timing of the subsequent stages open and subject to the achievements of the goals set for each stage. Interestingly, the committee felt that a single currency was not a necessary requirement for monetary union but a 'natural and desirable further development of the monetary union'.[5] Stage one represented the initiation of the process and included the completion of the internal market, the reduction of existing disparities through programmes of budgetary consolidation, more effective structural and regional policies, full financial integration and increased cooperation among central banks. Stage two would concentrate on the creation of the basic organs and structure of economic and monetary union and could begin only when a new EU treaty had come into force. In the economic field, the European Parliament and Council of Ministers would consolidate the single market and competition policy, strengthen structural and regional policies and further improve the coordination of macroeconomic policies by setting medium-term policy objectives, precise but not yet binding limits to government budget deficits and by assuming a more active role in the discussion of economic and exchange rate policies. In the monetary field, a 'European System of Central Banks' (ESCB) would be set up, absorbing the previously existing institutional monetary arrangements. The key task for this body would be to begin the transition from stage one (the coordination of independent national monetary policies by the Committee of Central Bank Governors) to the final stage (the formulation and implementation of a common monetary policy by the ESCB). The final stage would commence with the irrevocable fixing of exchange rates of national currencies, eventually leading to a replacement of the national currencies by a single community currency. From today's perspective, it is interesting to recall what the authors of the report thought necessary in the field of fiscal policy to make monetary union work:

> The rules and procedures of the Community in the macroeconomic and budgetary field would become binding. In particular, the Council of Ministers, in cooperation with the European Parliament, would have the authority to take directly enforceable decisions, i.e., to impose constraints on national budgets to the extent to which this was necessary to prevent imbalances that might threaten monetary stability; to make discretionary changes in Community resources (through a procedure to be defined) to supplement structural transfers to Member States or to influence the overall policy stance in the Community; to apply to existing Community structural policies and to Community loans (as a substitute for the present medium-term financial assistance facility) terms and conditions that would prompt member countries to intensify their adjustment efforts.[6]

These provisions represented a much deeper infringement on national sovereignty than eventually agreed in the Maastricht Treaty and the Stability and Growth Pact and foreshadowed the attempt of Chancellor Merkel at the EU summit of 9 December 2011 to insert binding rules for fiscal policy in the EU treaty.

How was it possible that French–Italian dissatisfaction with the EMS and the seemingly maverick initiative of a German foreign minister produced tangible progress towards monetary union? The answer to this question can be found in the changing power structure of Europe. When Mikhail Gorbachev took over as leader of the Soviet Union in 1985, East–West relations thawed and the Cold War started to die down. This again raised the question of Germany's position in a changed Europe: 'Unless we make progress in the construction of Europe, we will not escape bargaining over Germany between East and West', Mitterrand told his premier Chirac and his finance minister Balladur in early 1987.[7] Kohl agreed with Mitterrand's assessment and the German side proposed a Franco-German defence council. The idea was to create a joint decision-making process, especially with regard to French nuclear battlefield weapons, which in an armed conflict might be used on German soil. However, Mitterrand's adviser Jacques Attali shifted the focus from defence to monetary cooperation. Mitterrand was determined to push the idea forward. In talks with Spanish prime minister Felipe Gonzalez, he called for a common currency as a means to deal with the German issue. But he was under no illusion with regard to the problems he faced: 'Of course the Germans resist this... The Mark is the manifestation of German power. This is a very deep issue that transcends the reflexes of bankers and goes even beyond politics.'[8] Although one can only speculate today what might have happened, it seems indeed likely that mere disaffection with the asymmetric nature of the EMS and the desire to fortify the single market would not have been enough to induce the Germans to give up their beloved D-Mark.

The fall of the Berlin Wall in November 1989 reinforced Mitterrand's determination to bind Germany more firmly into the EU through the creation of a common currency. He had already told Britain's prime minister Margaret Thatcher in September 1989: 'In contrast to you, I see the perturbations in the East as one more reason to realise the [European] Union. Without a common currency, we are all of us – you and we – already subordinate to the German will.'[9] Meanwhile, in the eyes of the French, Kohl had turned lukewarm towards EMU and he incensed them further when on 28 November he unveiled a ten-point plan for German unification before the Bundestag. On 29 November, France's foreign minister Dumas declared in the National Assembly that France put special emphasis on Kohl's declaration that German reunification had to proceed in the context of European integration. On the following day, in a meeting with Genscher, Mitterrand called on Germany to agree to serious negotiations on EMU before the end of 1990. 'Otherwise, Mitterrand said – with a touch of melodrama – Germany risked a "triple alliance" between France, Britain and the Soviet Union that could isolate Germany in similar fashion to the eve of the First and Second World Wars.'[10]

In view of this threat Kohl gave in and agreed at the Strasbourg summit on 8 December 1989 to an intergovernmental conference on EMU: 'The European Council declares that on the basis of these decisions the first phase of EMU according to the schedule of the report of the Delors Committee can begin on July 1, 1990.'[11] Four days later, on 12 December, a somewhat exasperated Kohl told US foreign minister James

Baker in Berlin that he understood the concerns of other European countries about German unification, saying that already today Germany was economically the number one country in Europe. When 17 million Germans joined, this would create nightmares for several others. What more could Kohl do than to show support for the creation of economic and monetary union? He had taken this decision against German interests – even the president of the Bundesbank opposed this step – but it was politically important because Germany needed friends.[12]

Having regained full national sovereignty through unification and having been freed from the military threat emanating from the former Soviet Union, subsequent German governments began to lose their political deference to France and their other European partners and to behave like any other 'normal EU member state'. 'Normal' behaviour in the EU consisted more often than not of the pursuit of national interests within the EU without much regard for the common good of European unity. As long as Germany had been willing to protect the union by footing the bill for such behaviour, common European projects could be implemented relatively smoothly. When Germany closed its chequebook, progress towards 'ever-closer union' became more cumbersome. The change in the political relationship was also reflected in the change in personal relationships between the French and German political leaders. While Kohl and Mitterrand, in a highly emotional gesture, had held hands at a ceremony in a military cemetery in Verdun in 1984, the relationship between Jacques Chirac and Gerhard Schröder became less cordial and more businesslike. Thus, Chancellor Schröder's interest in the 'Third Way' of New Labour under Tony Blair caused serious irritation in Paris.[13] Relations turned sour when Schröder cancelled a joint event on Armistice Day on 11 November 1998. They deteriorated further when Schröder clashed with Chirac over payments to farmers under the Common Agricultural Policy at the Berlin summit of 1999 and over the future distribution of votes in the EU at the Nice summit of 2000. Relations only began to improve as of 2002, when both the president and the chancellor were unexpectedly returned to office in the elections of that year. Opposition to the Iraq War then united both leaders as of 2003 in a partnership of equals against the policies of the Bush administration. Relations between Chancellor Merkel and President Sarkozy also had a rocky start. Still in May 2010, almost two years after Sarkozy's election, the press delighted in the mutual animosity between the German chancellor and the French president.[14] However, the escalation of the euro crisis in 2010–12 eventually forced Merkel and Sarkozy to cooperate so closely in leading the EU that the press coined the name 'Merkozy' for the couple. Their relationship was a complete reversal of pre-unification French–German leader couples: she led, he followed. More generally, if the pre-unification French and German leaders saw unification as a question of war and peace, the post-unification leaders have looked at it more from the perspective of the political and economic advantages for their respective countries. The hierarchy in the relationship has increasingly reflected the economic power of the two countries instead of the military power balance after World War II. Most importantly, the initial inspiration for economic integration disappeared into thin air.

In 1990, the central council of the Bundesbank had already warned that a monetary union is 'an irrevocable joint and several community which, in the light of past experience, requires a more far-reaching association, in the form of a comprehensive political union, if it is to prove durable'. With these concerns in mind, negotiations for the new treaty began through two separate Intergovernmental Conferences (IGCs) – one dealing with monetary union, the other with political union. In April 1991, a draft set of treaties was presented at the Luxembourg European Council, after which extensive negotiations took place between national governments, leading to the signing of the treaty in the Dutch town of Maastricht on 7 February 1992. In the same month, the Bundesbank council admonished the politicians:

> The Maastricht decisions do not yet reveal an agreement on the future structure of the envisaged political union and on the required parallelism with monetary union. Future developments in the field of the political union will be of key importance for the permanent success of the monetary union.[15]

The so-called 'European federalists' in Germany shared the Bundesbank's concern that political union was needed to ensure the success of monetary union and exerted pressure on Kohl to move on with the political integration of Europe. In response to these pressures, he declared to the German Bundestag on 25 September 1992 in the wake of the referendum on the Maastricht Treaty in France:

> This progress in our view is not enough. Maastricht is only a first step in the right direction. We will have to work hard with some of our partners to convince them to materially improve the democratic control of the European institutions by a strengthening of the rights of the European Parliament in the coming years, but at the latest in the context of the intergovernmental conference planned for 1996.[16]

For the Germans, political union generally meant a federation of European states along the lines of the Federal Republic of Germany. Such a union required the surrender of significant parts of national fiscal sovereignty, which is at the core of political sovereignty, to a central authority. But, as Marjolin already observed in the 1950s, this was not the vision of the French and most other European leaders who held their national sovereignty in too high esteem to have it watered down in a European federation, particularly with regard to the right of parliament to decide over the government's budget. Hence, it is not surprising that the new intergovernmental conference that was to make up for the shortcomings of its predecessor produced only limited progress to a real political union. The results were encapsulated in the Amsterdam Treaty of 1997, which covered a wide range of issues from a common foreign and security policy to an improved decision-making process (by extending voting based on a 'qualified majority' to a larger number of decisions).[17] But the treaty did not touch national sovereignty in fiscal policy, an area where the Delors Report had demanded far-reaching political integration. In the wake of this shortcoming, the fledgling momentum of the early 1990s towards a political union with pooled sovereignty over government finances dissipated over the course of the decade.

Recognizing the impossibility of merging the sovereign states of Europe into a US- or German-style federal state, German foreign minister Joschka Fischer made a last effort to promote political union as a federation of states. In a speech at the Berlin Humboldt University in the spring of 2000 he reminded his audience that the European idea originated in the rejection of the concept of national sovereignty established after the peace of Westphalia in 1648.[18] The struggle of hegemony in Europe unleashed by this concept had in the event pushed Europe into the catastrophes of the twentieth century. Fischer suggested the sharing of sovereignty based on the principle of subsidiarity in a federation of European states. This could not be done through further piecemeal integration without a clear idea of the final state of Europe – the 'Monnet Method' – but required a new foundation for Europe based on a European constitution.[19] The latter was to define the boundaries between national and European sovereignty. Fischer expected the development to the final state of Europe over two or three steps in the course of the first decade of the new millennium. At the beginning stood enhanced cooperation of the EMU member states towards an economic union, followed by the conclusion of a new basic European treaty, the nucleus of a constitution, to be crowned by the full integration into a European federation. The declaration of Laeken of December 2001 indeed called on the EU to improve democracy, transparency and efficiency, paving the way for the establishment of a European convention with the mandate to draft a European constitution. But instead of opening a new chapter of European integration, these efforts only proved that the process of integration had come to an end. The treaty establishing a constitution for Europe was rejected in public referendums in 2005 in France and the Netherlands, two countries that had always been regarded as members of the avant-garde of European integration. Key elements of the constitution were rescued in a lower profile, technical treaty, named after the city of Lisbon, which was eventually adopted after some difficulties in 2009. A Charter of Fundamental Rights of the European Union, a key part of the constitution, was taken out and the treaty was given the low-key name of the 'Treaty on the Functioning of the European Union' (TFEU). These developments – symbolized by the downsizing of the name of the new EU treaty – suggest that the 'inner logic' of European integration, according to which political union was the necessary consequence of monetary union, has ceased to work.

Failure to establish a full political union with pooled sovereignty over government finances had a profound impact on the project of establishing a common currency. If in the past the creation of a common currency had been seen as a catalyst to create political union, it had now turned into an undertaking whose value was measured primarily in the economic advantages it would afford its members. As several studies and the test established by the Blair government to assess the benefits of EMU for the UK have indicated, such economic advantages are difficult to quantify in a cost–benefit analysis and hence can provide only a weak foundation for monetary union. Future historians may find it ironic that the threat of war disappeared before the process of European unification had found its fulfilment in political union, which had been seen as the key instrument to permanently eliminate the possibility of war in Europe. As a result, EMU, which originally should have been fortified by shared fiscal sovereignty in a political union, was caught out on a limb. During the 1990s, European leaders were warned that the creation of a monetary union without the prospect of a political union following in the not-too-distant future was risky business. Driven forward by the political momentum towards the EMU they had created, and shutting their eyes before the risks, they went ahead anyway.

Chapter 3

A History of Failures

'There is no example in history of a lasting monetary union that was not linked to one state.'

—Otmar Issing, former chief economist of the Bundesbank and the ECB, in 1991[1]

As was already pointed out in the Delors Report, the key feature of a monetary union is the common issuance of money through the locking of exchange rates. In principle, money can remain in national denominations. A common currency, then, is merely a desirable feature of a monetary union, not a necessary one. If we follow this characterization we can distinguish several historical forms of monetary unions among states: (1) the coordinated issuance of coins by national central banks or treasuries and mutual acceptance of these as means of payment; (2) the locking of exchange rates of national currencies against an agreed numéraire with the continued existence of central banks; (3) the creation of a single central bank responsible for the issuance of a common currency. In this chapter we shall take a look at the Latin and Scandinavian currency unions as examples of a monetary union of the first type. We shall then review the gold standard and its successor, the

US dollar standard under the Bretton Woods system, as examples of monetary union arrangements of the second type. In our review of monetary unions we shall finally turn to the Austro-Hungarian union and the post-Soviet ruble zone as an example of the third type. These unions all have disappeared and can be used to undertake a 'post-mortem' of currency unions. But what can we learn from monetary unions that survived by being bolstered through the creation of political unions? To review this experience we take a look at the experience of the German Reich. Moreover, the United States of the nineteenth century offers interesting lessons on how to deal with government finances in a federation of states. But before we go *in medias res*, a little health warning: since my intention was not to write a history book, some readers may find this chapter a bit sketchy; others may feel bothered by too much detail. My hope is, however, that a historical review will help the majority of readers to see that the creation of a monetary union without full political union is indeed a high-risk undertaking.

In 1865, France, Belgium, Italy and Switzerland created the so-called Latin Monetary Union (LMU). In the following four years seven more countries joined, including Spain and Greece. Participating countries exchanged their national coins against new standard coins minted from either silver or gold and exchangeable at a ratio of 4.5 grams of silver to 0.290322 grams of gold (i.e., at a ratio of 15.5 to 1). Coins in bronze and bank notes were not covered by the agreement of mutual acceptance but could be converted at official rates into the common coins. National treasuries were obliged from the beginning to accept payments in other member states' coins, while this only became obligatory for private citizens as of 1885. Efforts by national governments to fund fiscal deficits through the debasement of the common currency burdened the union from its beginning. An early and ruthless debasement of the common currency was initiated by the Papal States, which had been accepted as a member by the founding member countries of the LMU in 1866. Cardinal Giacomo Antonelli, the treasurer of the pope, saw membership in the LMU as a way to both maintain commercial relationships with Italy and to overcome the financial difficulties of the Vatican. Relying on the goodwill of the French government, Antonelli reduced the silver content of the coins and massively raised issuance. With a population of between 500,000 and 700,000, the Papal States issued as much diluted silver money as Belgium with a population of 5 million. The monetization of public debt had a positive effect on the finances of the Papal States but eventually led to the rejection of papal coins by France and Switzerland and the ejection of the Papal States from the LMU in September 1870.

Also, in 1866 Italy's budget came under pressure due to the war with Austria. The government borrowed funds from its national bank, which issued paper money against this. As the exchange rate between the nationally issued paper money and the common coins was fixed, Italy could augment the total money supply in the union and fund part of its war effort by imposing an inflation tax on all the members. In a similar exercise, during the Franco-German war of 1870–71 the French central bank began to issue an increased amount of paper money to secure the funding of government activities. While the official exchange rate of paper money and the common coins was fixed, the market exchange rate of French paper money declined against the common coins. As a result, coins were shipped to other member countries of the union and converted into paper money there at the official exchange rate, forcing an increase of the money supply across the union. This practice lasted until 1878 and induced a discussion on the dissolution of the monetary union. While it was generally agreed that coins could only be changed back in those countries where they had been minted, the discussions disclosed another problem. Belgium had struck huge amounts of silver coins. As the market price for silver had constantly fallen during the 1870s, changing silver coins into gold coins or paper money at their official exchange rate in Belgium would have meant large losses for the Belgian treasury. Hence, Belgium pushed for a burden sharing among all member states of the union. It was agreed that silver coins would be changed into gold coins or paper money at the official exchange rate in the country of issuance, and that Belgium, together with Switzerland (which suffered from a similar problem), would receive compensation for the losses incurred in this trade. However, the agreement was never implemented as no one was prepared to make the compensation payments. In view of these problems, the minting of new silver coins was discontinued in 1878. From that year on, only gold coins were officially accepted as common currency but existing silver coins still circulated. As the price of silver, and hence the market value of silver coins, often differed from the exchange rate against gold coins set officially in each country, silver coins were shipped around to exploit arbitrage opportunities and were sometimes melted when the price of silver exceeded the denomination of the coins. This of course led to destabilising variations in the money supply.

Following the example of Papal States, Greece, which had joined the LMU in 1868, decreased the amount of gold in its coins and was ejected from the union in 1908. At the beginning of World War I, all LMU countries (except

Switzerland) printed more paper money. Accordingly, the market exchange rate for the paper money of France, Belgium and Italy depreciated vis-à-vis that of Switzerland. Again the depreciated paper money was exchanged at the more favourable exchange rate into silver coins, which were then shipped to Switzerland to be changed back into Swiss paper money. The result was higher inflation in Switzerland. In October 1920, frustrated by this money arbitrage, Switzerland declared the import and circulation of coins from other LMU countries illegal and replaced foreign silver coins still circulating within its borders with national silver coins. As LMU member states turned away from the issuance of metal coins and melted the existing stock during World War I, a large quantity of paper money remained in circulation after the war. As paper money did not have legal tender status outside the issuing country, the currency union no longer had any practical effect. The LMU officially ended in 1927, after Belgium (in 1926) and Switzerland (in 1927) had terminated the agreement on mutual acceptance of gold coins as legal tender.

On 18 December 1872, Sweden, Norway and Denmark established the Scandinavian Monetary Union (SMU) by fixing the exchange rates of their currencies at par to each other and at a rate of 0.403 grams of gold per krone (the common currency unit). In contrast to the LMU, where only gold and silver coins were accepted as legal tender, the SMU was based on free circulation and mutual acceptance of all (gold, silver and bronze) coins. The coins were issued by all three member states in the same denominations, fineness and metal content. From 1901 onwards, bank notes were also accepted at par to each other. Sweden, Norway and Denmark kept *de jure* sovereignty over their monetary policy. For example, there was no agreement on a common interest rate policy. Yet, from November 1885 onwards, even bills of exchange (drafts) were mutually accepted between the three central banks. In order to facilitate foreign trade and payments between the three countries, a mutual clearing agreement existed between the national central banks with mutual payment transactions and three-month credit facilities. The period from 1885 until the dissolution of the political union between Sweden and Norway in 1905 is regarded as the most successful phase of the SMU. When Sweden and Norway parted political company, the mutual agreement to change back gold coins between national central banks free of charge was terminated by Sweden. For a while, transaction fees higher than the costs for shipment of bank notes between the two countries were imposed. After 1905, expansionary monetary policy by Denmark and Norway led to a decoupling of market prices of paper money from contractually agreed parities. Similar to the dynamics outlined in the case of the LMU, arbitrage activities increased. Danish and Norwegian bank notes were taken to Sweden and exchanged for gold coins, which eventually returned to Denmark and Norway to be changed back into bank notes at the official rate. To avoid losing gold coins against debased Danish and Norwegian paper money, Sweden unsuccessfully tried to ban the export of gold. In the event, the continuous outflow of bank notes caused monetary scarcity in Denmark and Norway and led to an oversupply of money in Sweden.

With the outbreak of World War I, all three member states of the SMU suspended the gold convertibility of their bank notes and a mutual ban on gold exports was imposed. As of October 1915, Scandinavian central banks had ceased to mutually accept their bank notes at par. Due to different national monetary policies, the market exchange rates differed from the official exchange rates.

For example, Danish and Norwegian bank notes were accepted in Sweden only at a discount of 2.5 per cent and 1.25 per cent, respectively. The differences between official and market exchange rates for banknotes, and the fixity of banknotes to coins, provided arbitrage opportunities and induced the shipment of coins between countries to exploit these opportunities. In response, Sweden in 1916 refused to accept gold coins as legal tender. Five years later, in 1921, the free circulation of other coins among the Scandinavian countries was suspended, and in July 1923 all three central banks began a mutual exchange of their remaining stock of token coins. In 1924 regulations on the acceptance of coins and bank notes were suspended in all countries of the monetary union and monetary systems were renationalized. The formal end of the SMU came on 24 February 1924 when Denmark implemented a new currency act abolishing all provisions regarding coins within the SMU. As was the case for its Latin counterpart, insufficient monetary and fiscal discipline of its members brought the union to an end.

The history of fixed exchange rate systems – a weaker form of a currency union – was also not encouraging. During World War I, the gold standard (where the exchange rates of currencies were fixed against each other and gold) was suspended as countries used their money printing presses to finance the war effort. This led to inflation at varying degrees. When countries returned to the gold standard after the war, they did so without properly taking into account the real exchange rate changes that had taken place during wartime due to differences in inflation rates. Some countries even returned to the system at pre-war gold parities. As a result of real exchange rate misalignments, severe disparities in balance-of-payments emerged during the 1920s. France and the US both accumulated large gold reserves thanks to their balance-of-payments surpluses while the UK and Germany saw their reserves melt away on the back of deficits that needed to be financed. The problem was especially acute in Germany, which had to rely on short-term borrowing in the international capital market – a significant part of it in foreign currency – to fund its balance-of-payments deficit. As a result, German banks accumulated significant interest rate and foreign currency risks. In 1929, the big banks in Berlin funded 97 per cent of their total borrowing needs with short-term instruments, and relied on foreign creditors for 38 per cent. When the short-term capital flows began to dry up in the wake of the 1929 stock market crash and the 1930 elections, where the Nazi Party (NSDAP) reached a share of 18 per cent of the votes and became the second largest political force in the Reichstag, Germany experienced a balance-of-payments crisis. Deprived of their short-term funds, the commercial banks attempted to shrink their balance sheets by reining in credit. Since credit had been extended longer-term and share portfolios had declined in value, this created great difficulties. Bank equity and profits shrank.

The crisis reached a new dimension on 11 May 1931, when Creditanstalt (CA), the largest Austrian bank, reported a loss that wiped out almost its entire equity capital. This triggered a bank run that abated only when news came out that the Austrian central bank would obtain a credit from abroad in the amount of 150 million Austrian shillings, 10 million more than the loss reported by CA. By that time, however, confidence had been severely damaged. Foreign investors feared that the collapse of CA would have disastrous knock-on effects to other banks in Austria and Germany. News of big losses at Karstadt (a German retailer) also on 11 May, and at Nordstern (an insurance company) a little later on 30 May, reinforced the panic unleashed by CA. In consequence, foreign investors withdrew some 288 million Reichsmark (RM) from German banks alone in the month of May. The renewed budgetary efforts of the Brüning government and the rejection of further war reparation payments induced foreign creditors to fear state bankruptcy, leading them to withdraw even more funds. Between 1–17 June the Reichsbank lost 1.4 million RM, more than half of its stock of foreign reserve in the form of gold and foreign currency. As a result, reserves came close to the lower limit of 40 per cent of money in circulation required under the Young Plan and induced the Reichsbank to raise interest rates to rein in growth. On 17 June, Nordwolle – Europe's biggest wool company – reported a huge loss. Subsequently it was discovered that the CEO had forged accounts to hide losses from financial speculation, and the company collapsed. This caused a series of bank runs, most prominently on Danat and Dresdner Bank, leading to bank holidays on 14–15 July. In the following months, large parts of the German banking sector had to be totally or partially nationalized to restore its capital base.

The experience of Germany in the early 1930s highlights the importance of a lender of last resort in a fixed exchange rate system. As the crisis unfolded and the Reichsbank lost foreign exchange reserves, its president Hans Luther knocked in vain on the doors of the Bank of England, the US Federal Reserve, the Bank of France, and the Bank for International Settlement to obtain emergency credits. Without these funds, the Reichsbank was forced to raise the discount rate to 15 per cent in mid-July 1931 and induce a severe credit crunch in the midst of recession. The consequences of the banking crisis for the real economy were severe. In significant part owing to the credit crunch,

German real GDP fell in 1932 to only 65 per cent of its level in 1928 and the number of unemployed surged to 5.6 million or 29.9 per cent of the dependent labour force. The economic and social crisis played an important role in the takeover of government by the NSDAP in 1933.

After World War II, the Western powers replaced the pre-war gold standard with a fixed (but adjustable) exchange rate system, the so-called Bretton Woods system, where the US dollar performed the role of the monetary anchor. Mindful of the catastrophe in the early 1930s under the gold standard, the architects of the Bretton Woods system aimed for a monetary regime that fostered free international trade, ensured price stability and was capable of assistance to countries in need of external economic adjustment. Disparity in countries' balance-of-payments should never again lead to financial crises, protectionism and economic collapse. At the founding conference, held in 1944 at the American resort Bretton Woods, two blueprints for the new monetary system competed. The first came from John Maynard Keynes, the chief negotiator for the UK Treasury. Keynes suggested that member countries of the system should maintain parity of their currencies against a global reserve currency, which he named the 'bancor'. A world central bank was to issue the bancor and determine the global money supply. To correct disparity in balance-of-payments, both surplus and deficit countries were supposed to take adjustment action. Thus, Keynes saw the need to distribute the adjustment burden between debtor and creditor countries and avoid asymmetric pressure on debtor countries alone. Such asymmetry had clearly contributed to the adjustment failure in the early 1930s. However, the US government had little sympathy for symmetric rules. It was clear that the US would emerge as the dominating military, political and economic power from World War II. Moreover, the US would also be a major creditor country to the rest of the world. The US government did not want to be told what to do by an international central bank staffed by representatives of weakened European powers. Hence, Harry Dexter White, the chief international economist of the US Treasury, presented an alternative scheme in which the US dollar – backed by the gold reserves of the US government – would be the anchor currency of the system, and in case of imbalances the burden of adjustment would lie on the side of the country with a balance-of-payments deficit.[2] Although in the event White compromised on a few points with Keynes, his plan was eventually adopted by the conference. Indeed, any new scheme would have been stillborn without the full backing of the US.

In the regime officially established on 27 December 1945, the 29 participating countries were required to maintain their exchange rate within a fluctuation margin of 1 per cent against the US dollar. The US government committed to exchange the US dollar into gold at a price of USD 35 per ounce, which had been established by Roosevelt in 1934 after an earlier hefty devaluation of the dollar. Instead of a world central bank, the International Monetary Fund (IMF) was to police the system. Its task was to monitor the policies of the member countries and advise governments and central banks on how to ensure external balance and exchange rate stability. Any exchange rate change versus the dollar beyond the 1 per cent fluctuation margin required IMF approval. To be able to provide temporary financial assistance to countries in need of external adjustment – and hence to prevent a 1930s-type balance-of-payments crises – the IMF was endowed with reserve funds. Member countries were assigned 'quotas' based on their population size and economic power in a pool of total funds, initially USD 8.8 billion. Based on their quotas, members had to pay a subscription into the fund, consisting of a 25 per cent share payable in gold or currency convertible into gold (i.e., the dollar at the time of foundation) and a 75 per cent share payable in their own national currency. In case of payment problems, member countries were allowed to draw on 25 per cent of their quota and, in case this amount proved to be insufficient, request additional loans in foreign currency. With this, temporary balance-of-payments deficits could be covered without the need to induce a monetary contraction leading to deflation and economic downturn, as had been customary under the gold standard. The effects of permanent changes in international competitiveness on balance-of-payments could be neutralized by occasional changes in the par value of currencies against the dollar. However, since the US had been running large trade surpluses after the war and most European countries had large deficits, there was a shortage of dollars, which the IMF (or its sister organization, the World Bank or, more accurately, the International Bank for Reconstruction and Development) could not relieve. Consequently, the US provided substantial financial aid to Europe mostly through grants awarded by the European Recovery Program (better known as the Marshall Plan, after its key proponent, US secretary of state George Marshall). Thanks to the outflow of dollars from this programme and through other channels, the US ran balance-of-payments deficits as of 1950, supplying dollars as international reserves to the other members of the Bretton Woods system.

In the years that followed, it became apparent that the system was inherently unstable: it required the US to run balance-of-payments deficits so as to ensure an adequate supply of international reserve currency and allow countries to grow, while the printing of dollars to fund the continuous US deficits risked undermining confidence in the dollar as a means to store financial wealth. This problem was first identified in 1960 by the economist Robert Triffin and accordingly dubbed 'Triffin's Dilemma'. As the international supply of dollars increased and drove the market price of gold up, foreign central banks tended to exchange their dollars against gold at the official price of USD 35 per ounce, leading to an outflow of gold from the US. Developments came to a head towards the end of the 1960s when the administration of Lyndon B. Johnson relied on monetary funding by the US Federal Reserve to pay for the war in Vietnam, in addition to its domestic social policies in the context of the so-called 'Great Society' programme. As more and more dollars were printed and flowed abroad to cover military expenses, the gold coverage of the money stock dropped from 55 per cent to 22 per cent in 1970. President de Gaulle of France was especially active in exchanging the dollar reserves of the Bank of France at the official price into gold, creating an accelerating drain on US gold reserves. In response, on 15 August 1971, US president Nixon imposed wage and price controls for 90 days and a 10 per cent import surcharge. Most importantly, he ended the official link of the dollar to gold and stopped the outflow of gold from the US. Subsequent attempts to restore the gold link to the dollar, most notably the so-called Smithsonian agreement of December 1971, all failed and the dollar price of gold surged (see Chart 3.1). Thus, in February 1973, the Bretton Woods system was disbanded and replaced by a system of freely floating exchange rates. With the end of the dollar–gold link in 1971, the global monetary system lost a hard, material anchor and turned into a fiat money system, where the supply of money is at the sole discretion of central banks.

Chart 3.1. Price of gold

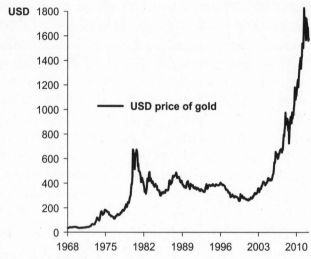

Source: Haver Analytics

The monetary unions or quasi monetary unions we have discussed so far had in common that money issuance at the national level was supposed to be coordinated in a way that satisfied all members. As we have seen, a lack of coordination from the beginning eventually dealt a deathblow to the unions, albeit after impressively long periods of time. One conclusion that could be drawn from these historical experiences is that money issuance should be centralized in order for the union to last. Unfortunately, history suggests that this is not enough. What is also required is strict fiscal discipline. However, it is very rare to find this in unions of sovereign states. The example of the Austro-Hungarian monetary union can perhaps be regarded as the exception that proves the rule. Between 1867 and 1918, the Habsburg Empire consisted of two states, Austria and Hungary, each of which enjoyed a high degree of national sovereignty.[3] They had their own parliaments and governments and, most importantly from our perspective, issued their own national debt. However, they had a shared monarchy, army, foreign policy, legal system and currency. The Austrian National Bank issued the Austrian silver gulden, the official legal tender of the whole empire. Originally, the Austrian National Bank was a private institution under government charter, established at the end of the Napoleonic wars. It remained the country's sole central bank when Austria's governance structure was transformed from the Austrian Habsburg Empire into the Austro-Hungarian dual monarchy (the 'Compromise' of 1867) after Austria's defeat by Prussia in the 1866 war.

For the first 23 years, the national bank, which became the Austro-Hungarian Bank in 1878, issued paper money backed by silver reserves. However, with a fall in the market price of silver leading to monetary instability, the bank received a new charter in 1887, which set the stage for a switch to a quasi gold standard. The switch took place gradually. In 1892 a new gold-based currency, the crown, was introduced. In the second stage, other coins in circulation lost their status of legal tender and as of 1900 the crown became the sole legal tender in the empire. In order to build up the gold reserves to cover 40 per cent of the outstanding paper money, the governments of Austria and Hungary repurchased outstanding notes against gold, with 70 per cent of the cost covered by Austria and 30 per cent by Hungary, and paid the proceeds into the Austro-Hungarian Bank. With the move to the gold standard, the bank asserted greater independence from the governments, strictly limiting advances to the treasuries so as to maintain the value of the paper money against gold. To keep the peg to gold stable, the bank steered the money supply through open market operations, buying or selling Austro-Hungarian bills.

Under the compromise that established the dual monarchy, a two-tier fiscal system was established with a 'confederate' and a 'country' level. The former received custom receipts and, as a supplement, transfers from the country budgets to fund its expenses, the lion's share of which went to the army. Deficits and debt issuance were not allowed at this level. At the country level, the governments were sovereign in deciding on spending, revenues and debt issuance to fund deficits. Following increases in the debt ratios during the first phase of the union, with Austria's debt surging from 55 per cent of its GDP in 1875 to 80 per cent in the early 1890s and that of Hungary jumping from 70 per cent to 120 per cent during the same period, difficulties raising new funds in the capital market induced a change in fiscal behaviour. By 1913, the debt ratios of Austria and Hungary had been brought down to 60 per cent and 70 per cent, respectively.

Debt reduction did not come at the cost of reduced growth. During 1895–1913, average per capita GDP growth was 1.5 per cent per year, more than twice the 0.7 per cent rate of the two preceding decades and similar to the growth rates of France or Sweden. The costs of the war of 1914–18 were largely funded through the money printing press. Following defeat, the dual monarchy fell apart. While parts of its territory went to existing states, five new states emerged: Austria, Hungary, Czechoslovakia, Romania and Yugoslavia. Although it was agreed that the successor states would stamp Austro-Hungarian bank notes circulating in their areas and then issue their own notes within a year, it took until 1920 for the monetary union to be completely unwound. As the successor states imposed various levies for the stamping, there was widespread forgery of stamps and smuggling of unstamped notes into territories with lower charges for stamping. In particular, Hungary and

Poland – as the last major countries to stamp the common notes – ended up with a massive acceleration of inflation rates caused by an inflow of unstamped notes from other territories. Currency reform failed in both Hungary and Austria as large fiscal deficits forced the countries to print more money, leading to hyperinflation in the early 1920s. The successor states eventually created their own central banks and a liquidator for the Austro-Hungarian Bank was appointed in August 1920. The unwinding was completed in July 1924.

The fate of Austro-Hungarian monetary union highlights the importance of an independent central bank and the commitment of the participants to fiscal discipline. The union worked best in 1895–1913, when the central bank maintained parity of the currency against gold and the member states reduced their debt. The seeds of its destruction were laid by the monetary funding of war expenses. This and the political disintegration after defeat destroyed the basis for the union and led to its breakup.

A further example of the need for monetary and fiscal discipline and a strong political commitment to monetary union is the fate of the ruble zone, which emerged after the breakdown of the Soviet Union in December 1991.[4] The dissolution of the Soviet empire left the newly independent countries in a state of political and economic instability. Most of the countries were more or less going through the same painful transformation from centrally planned to market economies. Not all of the countries adopted the structural reforms needed for this with equal pace. While the Baltic states transformed their political and economic systems quite quickly, others (like Uzbekistan, Kazakhstan and Belarus) lagged far behind, especially regarding the political transformation to a democratic system. The central bank of the newly created monetary union, despite some change, still reflected the old Soviet system. There, cash had been used only for payments between citizens, while book money had been used exclusively for payments between the central bank's branches and enterprises.

After the collapse of the Soviet Union, the central bank of the USSR, Gosbank, split into fifteen central banks, with the Central Bank of the Russian Federation (CBRF) still having the sole power to print cash in the form of rubles. The other central banks, however, controlled the creation of book money by extending credit. A lack of coordination within this structure allowed the individual central banks to lend to enterprises in their country at their own discretion, which led to an excess supply of book money and, in combination with price liberalization in 1992, a rise of inflation in the entire monetary union. The CBRF failed to meet the rising demand for cash in member countries, resulting from the expansion of book money. As a consequence, in late 1991 and early 1992, the three Baltic countries and the Ukraine suffered acutely from cash shortages. Perhaps the open intention of these states to gradually leave the ruble zone contributed to the supply shortages created by the CBRF. In response, the affected countries introduced parallel currencies in their territories: karbovanetz in the Ukraine, talonai in Lithuania, Latvian ruble in Latvia and Belarusian ruble in Belarus. Estonia, on the other hand, accelerated its preparations for introducing its own currency.

To regain control over inflation and to design a consistent monetary policy for the whole union, the member states held a conference in May 1992. Central bank representatives from all fifteen republics and the IMF participated but a solution to the problems remained elusive. Estonia then decided to leave the ruble zone and, against the recommendations of the IMF, introduced its own currency (the kroon) in June 1992. The kroon was pegged at a rate of 8:1 to the German mark by a currency board. The exchange rate to the ruble was set at 10:1 for a limited amount of notes and 50:1 for the remainder. Consequently not all rubles were exchanged for the new currency and currency migration – similar to that in the dying days of the Austro-Hungarian monetary union – took place. Estonian rubles found their way to neighbouring countries, especially to Russia, and led to surging inflation there. Encouraged by the positive development of the Estonian currency reform, Latvia (July 1992), Lithuania (October 1992) and the Ukraine (November 1992) subsequently introduced their own national currencies. However, inflation began to threaten the economic reform program of the Russian government, inducing political tensions between Russia and the other ex-Soviet republics. Against this background, the CBRF stopped the acceptance of book rubles coming from other countries and, from July 1992 onwards, demanded from the other member states the establishment of correspondence accounts for their payments with the CBRF. With this, the CBRF ended the convertibility of the book ruble in Russia.

Due to the strong negative reaction from other governments, this policy was later softened through the granting of credits by the Russian government and the CBRF to the republics in need. When the Ukraine exited the union in 1992 there were still eleven countries left that, with the exception of Azerbaijan, more or less declared their intention to stay in the union. During the conference in Bishkek in October 1992, the remaining member states of the ruble zone tried to establish an institutional structure for a sustainable monetary union. However, since the countries could not agree on the establishment of a congruent central bank system with a common monetary policy, the conference failed. A mere six member states (Russia, Kazakhstan, Armenia, Kyrgyzstan, Uzbekistan and Belarus) signed a vague treaty proclaiming stronger coordination of their monetary policy. The situation in late 1992 and early 1993 was characterized by deep uncertainty regarding the future of the ruble zone. In May 1993, Kyrgyzstan, encouraged by the example of Estonia and supported by the IMF, announced its exit from the ruble zone. Due to the further inflow of rubles and the lack of any agreement on the monetary union, Russia left the ruble zone only two months later in July 1993. Subsequently, the CBRF ceased to print Soviet rubles and started operating the new Russian ruble. Russian citizens had the right to exchange a limited amount of old ruble banknotes (35,000) into the new Russian ruble; the rest of the banknotes were to be deposited into a bank account for six months. With this, the Russian government sought to absorb the growing purchasing power of the Russian citizens and to stop the inflow of old rubles from other republics. After protests from Russian citizens, the exchange amounts for the old ruble were increased and the exchange period prolonged. Alongside the currency reform, Russia made a proposition to the remaining states to supply them with new rubles under the condition of their effectively complete subordination to the Russian monetary policy.

All republics were to give up their right to money creation to the CBRF. Since Georgia, Azerbaijan, Moldavia and Turkmenistan were already preparing their exit from the union, they rejected the Russian proposal. Armenia, Kazakhstan, Tajikistan, Uzbekistan and Belarus, however, were ready to accept these conditions and willing to conduct further talks. The reason for their readiness to compromise can be explained to some extent by their internal political situation: Uzbekistan and

Kazakhstan were still governed by autocratic Soviet-time leaders. Armenia was engaged in a military conflict with Azerbaijan, and Tajikistan was mired in civil war. Belarus proceeded rather slowly towards political and economic reforms. After subsequent talks it became clear that the Russian conditions were difficult to meet even for those five countries. Russia demanded that member states of the new union transfer their foreign currency and gold reserves to Russia to obtain Russian ruble banknotes. Lack of trust on both sides induced the remaining countries to drift away from the union, with Tajikistan being the last to leave in May 1995.

Our post-mortem of failed unions has pointed to a lack of monetary and fiscal discipline as a key reason for fragility. When political disunity coupled with the lack of economic discipline, the unions dissolved. The corollary to these observations would be that initially loose monetary arrangements only turned into more stable currency zones when economic discipline and political unity were strengthened. The creation of the German Reich and the United States of America in the course of the nineteenth century would seem to demonstrate this.

Following the defeat of Napoleon, the German Confederation was founded in 1815, with Austria and Prussia not only the most powerful members but also the strongest rivals.[5] The association was fairly loose and put very few constraints on members' policies. However, within this confederation, a subgroup of states embarked upon a journey of much closer integration. In 1834, a number of German states created a free trade zone, named the German Zollverein. Austria, Lübeck, Bremen, Hamburg, Schleswig-Holstein and Liechtenstein chose not to join. Four years later, in 1838, the member states of the Zollverein harmonized the German coinage system in the Dresden Coinage Convention. Before this, the political borders of the different principalities, each of which had its own coin system, divided Germany's monetary arrangements. However, most of these systems had been based on silver coins that had no common measure, weight or metal content. The 'gulden' dominated the south of Germany; the 'thaler' dominated the north.

The Dresden Coinage Convention introduced fixed exchange rates between the different silver coins circulating in the German territories, with the gulden–thaler exchange rate fixed at one thaler for 1.75 gulden. Furthermore, the convention set a fixed silver–copper ratio for coinage and forced the member states to make a choice between gulden and thaler as legal tender for their territories. In view of their limited use, banknotes were not included in the regulations. In addition, a new common coin – the 'Vereinsmünze' – was introduced. The coin was worth 2 thaler or 3.5 gulden. Due to its high value, however, it didn't play an important role in the daily monetary exchange. The next step towards monetary unification was taken with the Vienna Coinage Treaty of 1857, in which Austria fixed the exchange rate of its currency, the Austrian gulden, to both the thaler and the German gulden. However, the Austrian monetary link ended abruptly with the Austro-Prussian war of 1866. Nonetheless, the Vienna Coinage Treaty was important for two further reasons. Firstly, as the first ever international monetary treaty, it regulated the usage of paper money. Austrian banknotes, which were inconvertible into species, were banned from the payment system of the union. Secondly, the treaty introduced a uniform gold coin, the Vereinshandelsgoldmünze, which could only be used for foreign trade transactions. Owing to fears of turning the monetary arrangement into a bimetallic standard, the conversion of the gold coin into silver was prohibited.

The rivalry between Austria and Prussia culminated in the war of 1866, in which Prussia prevailed. As a consequence, Prussia annexed Schleswig-Holstein and other minor German territories. In addition, the German Confederation was dissolved and in its place Prussia created the North German Confederation. Its constitution of 1867 required member states to undertake a currency reform, which also regulated the circulation of banknotes in the entire territory. Over time, the need to regulate paper money became more pressing due to the progress of the trade intensification, hence the growing importance of paper money for financial transactions. In 1870 the North German Federation introduced a series of laws, which among other things prohibited the establishment of new note-issuing banks and regulated the issuing of paper money within the federation. The crucial step towards full political and economic integration of the German states was reached in the wake of the Franco-Prussian war in 1871. The southern German states, such as Bavaria, Baden and Württemberg, had already joined the North German Confederation during the war and, after its successful conclusion in July 1871, the German Reich was founded. Political unification led to a major currency reform in the years 1871 and 1873, with the aim of creating a modern, uniform currency system based on the gold standard. The new, gold-backed mark was divided into 100 pfennigs in line with the increasingly popular decimal system, and the old silver coins were fixed against it (at 3 marks for 1 Prussian thaler and 1.71 marks for 1 southern gulden). In order to ease acceptance of the currency reform, both thaler and gulden were very gradually removed from circulation. The reform of 1873 also regulated the use of paper money within the empire. It set the lowest par value for the newly denominated banknotes at 100 marks and ordered the withdrawal of the old banknotes by 1876. In addition, all paper money formerly issued by the German states was to be withdrawn. Both measures aimed for the further reduction of paper money in circulation. Since the removal of paper money would have been too strenuous, a further reform in 1874 provided that the old state paper money, at the nominal value of 184 million marks, be replaced by the new Reich treasury notes (Reichskassenscheine), with a face value of 120 million marks. Each state received a fixed amount of Reichskassenscheine (with denominations of 5, 20 and 50 marks) corresponding to its population. The remaining amount of paper money had to be covered by each state itself.

The final reform of the monetary system came in 1875–6, when the central bank of Prussia was transformed into the Reichsbank, which took over as the central bank of the German Reich. In the first three decades of its existence, the expenditures of the central authority were largely funded with income from postal and telegraph services, customs duties and contributions from the states. Efforts of the central government to introduce a federal tax were unsuccessful. Although the German Reich was able to live comfortably within its means in the early years of its existence, fiscal discipline eroded in the longer run. Both the Reich and the states eventually increased their debt levels dramatically. Total public debt rose from 37.4 per cent of net national product in 1880 to 62.7 per cent in 1913. In that year, 16 per cent of total debt was accounted for by the Reich, 51 per cent by the states and 33 per cent by the municipalities. The centre (the Reich) was in continuous conflict with the states over access to funding.[6] The latter were not willing to give the Reich sufficient fiscal power and therefore forced it to finance its expenditures (fuelled also by the arms race among the great European powers) through debt. The debt of the states rose in part due to the new responsibilities in the area of public policy. A major tax reform was blocked by the states in the fear that it would diminish their revenues and strengthen the Reich, a position supported by the major industrial interest groups. As a result, nationwide and sustainable tax reform remained elusive until World War I.

The effects of the malfunctioning of fiscal federalism on the German economy were severe. Germany had to pay higher long-term interest rates on its debt than other countries with higher debt to GDP ratios than Germany. Moreover, in order to ensure access to funding, the government limited capital exports with the result that Germany had the smallest flow of net foreign investment in Europe. The failure of the fiscal system laid the ground for an expansionary monetary policy by the Reichsbank, which ended in a period of hyperinflation in the 1920's. The British historian Niall Ferguson has argued that the conflict over distribution between the Reich and the states was one of the factors that pushed Germany into World War I.[7] Because the Reich was not able to obtain the funds necessary to compete successfully in the arms race with the powers of the Triple Entente, the political leadership was willing to strike before it had lost the race.

There is much to be learnt from the United States in terms of fiscal discipline across a fairly diverse economic area without the help of a money printing press. Between 1776, when it declared its independence, and 1790, the US government was effectively bankrupt and in default on most of its debt incurred during the War of Independence.[8] The new country had no banking system, functioning securities market or national currency, and the federal government had to rely on the thirteen states to collect and share the scarce tax revenue. Following the inauguration of George Washington as the first US president in April 1789, Alexander Hamilton, the first secretary of the treasury, set out to change this. He established the Bank of the United States, the mint and the securities markets. Moreover, he devised a scheme for dealing with the outstanding debt of USD 25 million, which was transferred to the federal government and added to its debt in the amount of USD 55 million. At USD 80 million, the total debt of the US was quite large, considering that GDP amounted to just USD 187 million in 1790. Hamilton defended his plan against much criticism, most notably from Thomas Jefferson, the secretary of state. He argued that it would align the issuance of debt with tax receipts (securing revenue from tariffs for the federal government), create a federal debt market and financial system and bind the states into the union. Of course, Hamilton's assumption of state debt by the federal government may well have pushed the latter into default if its position as debtor had not been strengthened by its access to the issuance of money through the Bank of the United States and the mint.

Implementation of the scheme was accompanied by political controversy and high drama, concerning among other things fairness between states with different debt levels, and led to a split of the political scene into 'Federalists' led by Hamilton and 'Democratic Republicans' led by Jefferson and James Madison. Perhaps more importantly, the bailout of states established a precedent and created a substantial moral hazard. Thus, the federal government had to assume again the debt of all states after the war of 1812 and the debt of the District of Columbia in 1836. Hamilton had hoped that the states would no longer issue debt after the assumption in 1790 and indeed, except during the war of 1812, this was more or less the case. The role of state governments was quite limited and funded mostly through land sales and bank charters.

But the development of the western states during the 1820s and 1830s created the need for infrastructure. Hence, the states borrowed to build canals or turnpikes, expecting to recoup the costs through tolls. However, in the wake of the financial panic of 1837 (which followed reckless bank lending and speculation after President Jackson refused to renew the charter of the US National Bank in 1836) and during the recession of 1839–43, a number of states could no longer service their debt. They petitioned Congress to assume their debt, as had been done before. Their creditors, mostly British and Dutch investors, also exerted pressure on the federal government to bail the states out, cutting it off from further lending in 1842. But Congress rejected the petition for debt assumption and gave four grounds for its action. First, the debt had been issued to fund state rather than federal projects; second, US banks held only a few state bonds and default would not create a systemic crisis; third, the deeply indebted states were a minority; and fourth, the US economy was sound enough to manage without foreign capital that would no longer flow in case of default. As a result, eight states and Florida (at the time still a 'territory') defaulted on their debt. This decision from 1842 established a 'no bailout' policy of states by the federal government as the norm. Thus, while no request for a bailout had been denied before 1840, no such request has been granted since. In the 1840s and 1850s, most US states adopted balanced budget amendments to their constitutions or similar provisions in their state law, contained their deficits and brought down their debt. Still, there were a number of state defaults in the following period (e.g., after the Civil War in the 1860s and during the Great Depression of the 1930s). The last state default occurred in 1933, when Arkansas was unable to make payments on highway bonds it had issued. The exception to the rule is the District of Columbia – not a state in the proper sense – for which the federal government managed the budget for four years during the 1990s and restored sound city finances.

Over the years, federal states occasionally bailed out cities or municipalities – most famously New York City in 1975 – but also let a considerable number go bust. Reflecting the policy of no-bailout, state debt has been contained at relatively low levels (e.g., in 2009 at 4.9 per cent of state GDP in Arizona, 7.3 per cent in California, 3.6 per cent in Nevada, 9.0 per cent in Illinois, 12.1 per cent in New Jersey and 11.2 per cent in New York) and poses no systemic risk for banks. Over the years, and especially after the Great Depression of the early 1930s, the role of the federal government in public finances and fiscal policy increased substantially. Today, federal spending accounts for about 60 per cent of total government spending, and the federal government pursues countercyclical policies during recessions through its own spending programme (e.g., unemployment insurance) or transfers to states, while the states often act in a procyclical manner. For our analysis, a key takeaway from the US experience is that only the threat of default seems to be a sufficiently strong motivator for fiscal discipline in largely sovereign entities that have no access to the money printing press. Bailouts give rise to moral hazard and tend to perpetuate themselves by creating the expectation that one's own financial mistakes will be corrected by others. The later US experience also shows how the rise of central government can create a dominating force in government finances and fiscal policy capable of materially influencing lower levels of government. However, the ascendancy of the US federal government to this role owes a lot to the specific historical experience of the Great Depression and may not have materialized in the same way without it.

An important conclusion from the brief history of past real or quasi monetary unions of sovereign states is that the build-up of severe fiscal imbalances in parts of the union, the monetization of these deficits, the emergence of balance-of-payments deficits among regions of the monetary arrangement and political disunion have been key reasons for failure. The disease leading to demise has been the build-up of excessive debt, mostly in the public but occasionally also in the private sector. As David Graeber has pointed out, debt crises have been a feature of economic and political life for thousands of years. In the very early times of the first agrarian empires (3500–800 BC), credit crises tended to be dealt with by debt forgiveness.[9] In modern times, money has been used to replace credit when trust had been lost due to overborrowing and default. When the stock of available money was fixed, as under the gold standard for instance, the scope for replacing credit relationships with money was limited and there was a need to annul these relationships through default. The economic consequences were often dramatic. The ability to create the additional money needed to replace credit when trust has been lost can soften the effects of widespread default. But this ability is also a great temptation to settle debt fraudulently by issuing untenable settlement promises through cheap money printing.

In general, the issuance of money has been the prerogative of governments and they have exercised their right through mints or central banks. Thus, the Bank of England, the second oldest central bank in modern history after the Swedish Riksbank, was created in 1694 to overcome the government's difficulties in raising money for the war against France. A company was created – named the Governor and Company of the Bank of England – with the purpose of borrowing GBP 1,200,000 and turning

the sum over to the government in return for receiving an
annuity of GBP 100,000 per year. The company could only
issue more debt with approval of Parliament. Against the
loan to the government, the company could issue 'bank
notes' over the same amount for commercial use. With
this arrangement the government, despite its low regard
in the eyes of investors, overcame the difficulties of raising
funds for the war.

A few decades before that time, in 1656, the king
of Sweden granted a charter to a businessman, John
Palmstruch, and his associates to establish the first bank in
Sweden. The bank borrowed 300,000 specie dalers against
bullion, merchandise, real estate and other valuables as
security, and extended loans to the king and other borrowers. It
took deposits of copper currency and issued certificates of
deposit – credit notes – which soon gained acceptance as
currency. Anticipating the technique of fractional reserve
banking, the bank soon issued more credit notes than it
had taken deposits. Payment difficulties occurred when
depositors wanted to withdraw their money in coins in
response to a rise in the price of copper. In 1664, the
government took over the bank, promised the redemption of
the notes in the future and in the meantime declared them
legal tender at their face value. Four years later, Palmstruch
was condemned to make up for the losses incurred by his
bank and threatened with a life sentence in case he did not
comply. At the same time, in September 1668, the bank was
placed under the authority and supervision of Parliament.
It was first named 'Bank of Estates of the Realm' and as of
1867, 'Riksbank'. In a humanitarian gesture, Palmstruch
was set free and pardoned in 1670. But he could not enjoy
his freedom for long as he died a year later.

The ability to create money and thus to obtain credit
unavailable by other means has always been a temptation

for governments in times of great need. But, as our historical survey has shown, it has been especially tempting in monetary unions of sovereign states. There, a state can obtain 'money credit' not only from its own citizens but also from those of the other states by unilaterally issuing more money. The incentive for a state to issue more money than its partners creates the risk of a competitive debasement of the common currency and hence makes currency unions of sovereign states inherently unstable. To avoid this problem, the issuance of money must be centralized. But this alone does not solve the problem of fiscal discipline. Member states may still overborrow in the hope that they will eventually be bailed out by other states or that their debt will be monetized by the common central bank. But how can fiscal discipline be enforced among largely sovereign public entities? In the US of the nineteenth century, where the federal government was still fairly weak, market forces eventually achieved this. The central authority was also fairly weak in the German Reich of 1870–1918 and there were no defaults of the member states. However, continuous fights over government revenue among the states, and between states and the central authority, led to an increase in debt at all levels of government. The results were higher interest rates and an accommodating monetary policy with eventually disastrous political and economic results.

Mindful of the past experience, the fathers of EMU wanted to shield the central bank from any pressures to monetize fiscal deficits and ensure fiscal discipline by holding countries responsible for their financial behaviour. Pressure for a hardening of the currency union came especially from Germany where painful memories of the monetization of government debt and the resulting hyperinflation have been passed on from generation to generation. To prevent the monetization of government debt, the European Central Bank (ECB) was prohibited from purchasing government bonds in the primary market and given far-reaching independence from government directions in the Maastricht Treaty that constituted EMU. To prevent excessive borrowing by governments, the Stability and Growth Pact was concluded with the goal of preventing governments from running up excessive fiscal deficits. Fines were envisaged to bring offenders back to the path of fiscal virtue. The threat of default was expected to exert further disciplinary influence on the conduct of fiscal policy. Countries should only join EMU when they met certain criteria: (1) government budget deficits should be no more than 3 per cent of GDP; (2) government debt ratios should be no more than 60 per cent of GDP (or on a clearly declining path if above this threshold); (3) inflation should be no more than 1.5 percentage points above the average of the three best-performing EU member states; (4) long-term interest rates should be no more than 2 percentage points higher than the average of the three EU states with the lowest inflation rates; and (5) candidate countries should have been members of the exchange rate mechanism (ERM II) under the European Monetary System (EMS) for two consecutive years and should not have devalued their currency during the period.

Although the entry criteria and the institutional safeguards against an erosion of EMU (along the lines of its historical predecessors) look impressive, there was no test as to whether prospective EMU member countries could keep their balance-of-payments in equilibrium by fulfilling the economic criteria for a common currency area. Robert Mundell argued in a groundbreaking article in 1961 that fixed exchange rates among different economic areas require a high degree of labour market mobility (or, as was later pointed out, a high degree of real wage flexibility). In a 1969 article, Peter Kenen suggested that fiscal transfers to some extent can make up for deficiencies in the real economy criteria for a fixed exchange rate regime (to which Kenen added a diversified production structure in each economic area).[10] In a union of sovereign states, in which members are banned from assuming each other's financial liabilities, interregional fiscal transfers have to, of course, be quite limited. In 2008, transfers among EMU member states amounted to only 0.1 per cent of GDP, compared to the interregional transfers equivalent of 2.3 per cent of GDP in the US.[11] Moreover, labour mobility among the prospective EMU member states was severely restricted due to language and administrative barriers. In 2008, only 0.18 per cent of the EU working population moved between member states, compared to 2.8 per cent in the US.[12] Firms were to a significant extent barred from laying off workers (see Chart 3.2), and none of the future EMU states exhibited the wage flexibility necessary to make up for limited labour mobility and employment flexibility. At the same time, these states had much more debt than, for instance, the federal states of the US, where debt ratios of state and local governments range from 7 per cent to 25 per cent of their respective GDP (2012 estimates). Perhaps the fathers of EMU did not trust the optimum currency area theory or they were naïve. Perhaps they thought that a thorough fulfilment of the Maastricht criteria for admission was a substitute, and maybe this might even have been the case had countries indeed fulfilled these criteria on a lasting basis, rather than in the mad dash to scrape over the hurdles that took place in reality. However, it is more likely that, in the tradition of the 'monetarists' (who believed that monetary integration would automatically lead to more real economic integration), they relied on the hope

Chart 3.2. Levels of employment protection

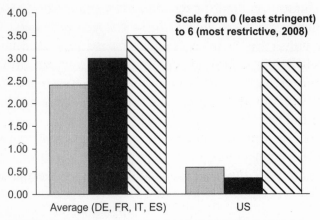

Source: OECD

that the necessary adjustments to the labour market and economy – or the interregional fiscal transfers – would be forced upon member countries automatically once EMU had begun. In the background, the hope may still have loomed that once monetary union was in place, political union would follow, despite the break in the 'inner logic' of European integration created by German unification and the end to the division of Europe.

While the neglect of optimum currency theory can perhaps be explained by the belief that conditions for a common currency area would fall into place after the start of EMU, the neglect of a robust financial architecture is more difficult to excuse. The prohibition of mutual bailouts by EMU governments and of monetization of government deficits by the ECB created the logical possibility of sovereign default in EMU. Yet, no arrangements to deal

with the risk of sovereign default were made. Financial
regulators and the ECB treated all sovereign debt in EMU
as risk-free. Banks did not have to set aside equity as a
risk buffer for their sovereign debt holdings and could
amass holdings beyond the limit of 25 per cent of their
balance sheet applied to other single-name credits. The
ECB did not differentiate between sovereign collateral
of different quality. There was no commonly funded
deposit insurance and no crisis management mechanism,
despite the experience with the role of the gold standard
during the Great Depression. At the time, questions with
regard to arrangements for financial crisis prevention and
management were left unanswered by the authorities.[13] In
retrospect, this behaviour can only be regarded as careless
in the extreme.

Chapter 4

The Euro's Happy Childhood and Its Abrupt End

'The Economic and Monetary Union and the euro are a major success. For its member countries, EMU has anchored macroeconomic stability, and increased cross-border trade, financial integration and investment. For the EU as a whole, the euro is a keystone of further economic integration and a potent symbol of our growing political unity. And for the world, the euro is a major new pillar in the international monetary system and a pole of stability for the global economy.'

—Joaquin Almunia, commissioner
for economic and monetary affairs, in 2008[1]

Not only did EMU begin without any visible technical glitches in 1999; it also functioned smoothly for almost a decade, seemingly defying optimum currency area theory and the considerable number of sceptics in the economics and financial profession. The ECB quickly gained respect among the eurozone population and participants in international financial markets, and the euro developed into

Chart 4.1. GDP growth in Euroland

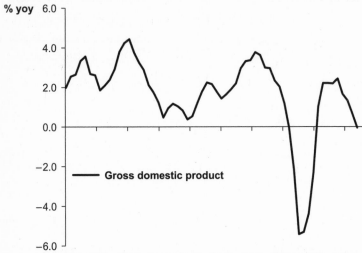

Source: Eurostat, Haver Analytics, Deutsche Bank Research

Chart 4.2. Inflation in Euroland

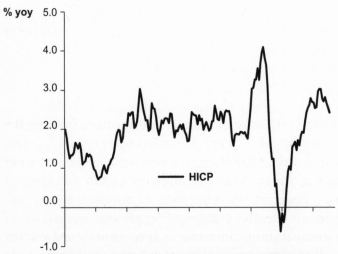

Source: ECB, Haver Analytics, Deutsche Bank Research

Table 4.1. Growth and inflation in key EMU member countries

	Growth			Inflation		
	1994–1998	1999–2007	2007–2011	1994–1998	1999–2007	2007–2011
Austria	2.5	2.6	1.4	1.6	1.7	2.2
Belgium	5.0	2.3	1.1	1.6	2.0	2.4
Finland	4.5	3.6	0.9	1.1	1.6	2.4
France	2.2	2.2	0.5	1.5	1.8	1.8
Germany	1.7	1.7	1.1	1.1	1.6	1.8
Greece	n/a	4.2	−0.6	5.9	3.2	3.3
Ireland	7.9	6.1	−1.0	1.8	3.4	0.8
Italy	1.9	1.5	−0.8	3.5	2.3	2.1
Netherlands	3.6	2.5	1.1	1.7	2.4	1.6
Portugal	4.4	1.8	0.0	3.2	2.9	1.8
Spain	3.6	3.7	0.3	3.3	3.1	2.4

Source: Eurostat, ECB, Haver Analytics, Deutsche Bank Research

the second-most important international reserve currency after the US dollar. With the notable exceptions of Germany and Italy, growth in most countries of the eurozone was buoyant and inflation extremely well behaved. This is illustrated in Charts 4.1, 4.2 and Table 4.1.

Owing to its lacklustre growth performance during the first few years of the euro, Germany was dubbed 'the sick man of Europe'. GDP growth averaged 1.7 per cent per year in 1999–2007, only marginally higher than that of Italy (1.5 per cent) and below that of Portugal (1.8 per cent). One reason for the disappointing growth was a lack of international competitiveness; it is commonly argued that this reflected the ambitious real exchange rate at the time of EMU entry. However, according to IMF calculations,

Germany's trade-weighted exchange rate, adjusted for relative unit labour cost developments, dropped by 8.0 per cent between the end of 1995 (when it had peaked) and January 1999 (when EMU began). It continued to fall until mid-2001, bringing the total decline since the end of 1995 to 18.6 per cent. Hence, it is fair to say that Germany's lack of competitiveness went beyond a temporarily distorted exchange rate. More likely, it was the legacy of the failure to implement long-overdue structural reforms.

In the early 1980s, when the governments of Ronald Reagan in the US and Margaret Thatcher in the UK embarked upon comprehensive market liberal reform, the government of Helmut Kohl felt that the German economy was in much better shape and hence only needed some marginal upgrading from its 1970s structure to be internationally successful. The fall of the Berlin Wall in 1989 and the unification of Germany in 1990 created high expectations for the future and distracted the Kohl government further from economic reform. The overheating of the economy in 1990–91, due to the boom of domestic demand unleashed by unification, induced the Bundesbank to sharply tighten monetary policy and plunged the economy into recession in 1992–3. Following its re-election in 1994, the Kohl government finally began to recognize the need for reform of the tax and social security system and the labour market. However, when the federal government finally began to move, political opposition by the majority of the Social Democratic Party (SPD)–led federal states in the Bundesrat, Germany's second chamber of parliament, blocked all initiatives. Oskar Lafontaine, leader of the SPD, had seized the opportunity to immobilize the federal government through the second chamber and make it look ineffective and helpless in the eyes of the voters. Lafontaine's political strategy paid off, and the

Kohl government was defeated in the federal elections of 1998. The coalition between the SPD and the Green Party, led by Chancellor Schröder, inherited an economy that was just beginning to be lifted by the Internet stock price bubble of the late 1990s. Thus, like its predecessor, the Schroeder government initially also failed to see the need for economic reform. However, this changed drastically when the economy plunged into recession following the burst of the Internet bubble. All of a sudden it became clear that Germany possessed an economy that was still running on an outdated 1970s platform. Taxes were higher, labour and product markets were more regulated and the social security system was more expensive and less efficient than in most of Germany's competitor countries that had benefited from economic overhaul during the 1980s. Companies were under pressure from more agile competitors, notably in the US and emerging market economies.

By 2003, Chancellor Schroeder became convinced that comprehensive economic reform was needed if Germany wanted to hold its position among the most advanced industrial countries. Consequently, he launched an economic reform programme, dubbed 'Agenda 2010'. The goal was to restore Germany's international competitiveness and improve the country's medium-term growth prospects for the new decade and beyond. It is probably no exaggeration to say that the agenda was Germany's most comprehensive economic reform and restructuring programme since the introduction of the 'Social Market Economy' by Germany's first and most-admired minister of economics, Ludwig Erhard, in the 1950s. Schroeder's agenda covered all aspects of the institutional framework of the economy. It included an overhaul of the tax system with a reduction in personal income and business taxes, a deregulation of the service sector that did not stop at the liberalization of Germany's infamous law setting shop opening hours, and an overhaul of the social security system, ranging from the welfare to the pension system and a reform of labour market regulations. While all measures were useful, it seems that the labour market reforms were the key to the restoration of the economy's international competitiveness. A tightening of unemployment and welfare benefits raised incentives to work while a liberalization of temporary and part-time work arrangements raised employment flexibility. In parallel, companies embarked upon a programme of raising economic efficiency. With the help of modern information and communication technologies and logistics, they separated production processes into different stages and located the respective stage in regions where they could be performed most cost efficiently. Thereby, German companies could profit from the opening up of Central and Eastern Europe and accession of Central European countries to the EU. A new generation of company and labour union leaders followed a more cooperative approach towards management–labour relations, which helped to increase flexibility at the company level. While the economic reforms and restructuring at the company level were overdue and essential for the subsequent strength and superior economic performance of the German economy, they initially depressed real disposable income growth, kept unemployment high and thus dampened domestic demand growth. The meagre growth that was achieved during these years was mainly based on exports, leading to a surge in Germany's current account surplus.

Outside Germany, living with the euro was initially mostly fun. In the run-up to the start of EMU, interest rates in the EMU candidate countries plunged to the

German level. Many citizens of the newly created euro area had never before in their lifetime seen interest rates as low as this. As creditors were rather indiscriminate with regard to the quality of borrowers during the inflation phase of the global credit bubble, private and public sector borrowers used the opportunity to generously load up on debt at what they regarded as rock-bottom interest cost. In some countries, notably Greece and Portugal, both the private and the public sector succumbed to the sweet temptation of easy credit and loaded the boat with debt. As the accumulation of public, but not private, debt was monitored by the European Commission in the context of the Stability and Growth Pact, Portugal was repeatedly reprimanded for its excessive public sector deficits and debt accumulation but was left undisturbed as far as private sector borrowing was concerned. Greece got off even more lightly as subsequent governments simply forged public deficit and debt statistics, a practice that had gained the country access to the exclusive club of euro countries in the first place. In other countries, prudence was not lost entirely. Thus, in Spain and Ireland, the public sector refrained from excessive borrowing and used the credit-driven growth of private sector activity and of associated tax payments to shrink deficits and reduce government debt. In Italy, on the other hand, the private sector remained a net saver despite the temptation of easy and cheap credit, while the government sector, in line with past practice, soon forgot its pledge of debt abstinence and indulged in renewed debt accumulation. Easy and cheap credit not only allowed debt-financed private and public consumption growth but also fuelled a boom in property prices, which in some countries, notably Spain and Ireland, led to strong and eventually excessive construction investment and overbuilding (Chart 4.3). Initial warnings

Chart 4.3. Nominal house prices

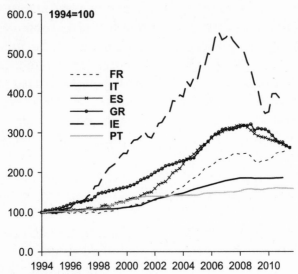

Source: BIS, Deutsche Bank Research

that membership of EMU was both a reward for financial and fiscal discipline and a challenge for both the private and public sector sounded distinctly hollow. Where was the punishment for inflexible labour markets and a lack of private and public financial discipline that had been predicted by academic economists? What did it matter that EMU had not been complemented by political union and associated interregional fiscal transfers? Cheap and easy credit from the international capital markets papered over any cracks that might have emerged soon after the start of EMU, in which only a few members were fit for the historical experiment of a lasting monetary union of sovereign states.

The ECB followed a two-pillar monetary policy strategy with a view to securing price stability, defined as consumer price inflation of less than 2 per cent, later modified to 'less

Chart 4.4. Euroland: 3-month interest rates and M3 money growth

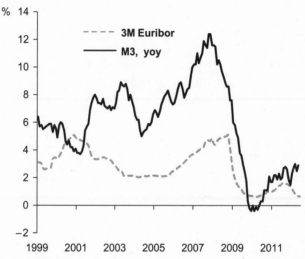

Source: ECB, Deutsche Bank Research

than but close to 2 per cent'.[2] In the first pillar, monetary developments were analysed and monitored. Broad money (M3) growth was assessed against a reference value deemed to be consistent with price stability over the medium-term (set at 4.5 per cent). In the second pillar, all relevant economic and price variables were analysed and monitored for the same purpose. From a cross-check of the analysis undertaken in both pillars, conclusions were drawn with regard to the course of monetary policy necessary to maintain price stability. The ECB liked to emphasize that its policy was directed at price stability for the union as a whole, disregarding the needs of specific countries. It was up to national authorities to adapt their policies so as to make them consistent with the common monetary policy. However, a closer look at its policy decisions shows that despite its stated strategy and proclaimed focus on

Chart 4.5. Euro area: Taylor rate vs. ECB main refi rate

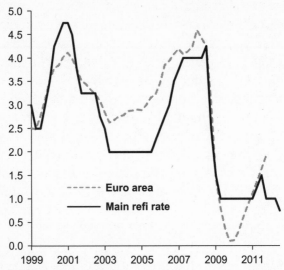

Source: Deutsche Bank Research

Chart 4.6. Germany: Taylor rate vs. ECB main refi rate

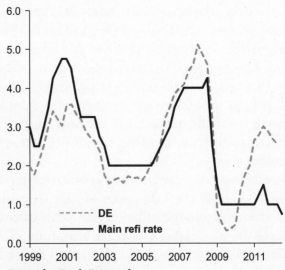

Source: Deutsche Bank Research

euro area aggregates, the ECB gave only minor attention to money growth and failed to set interest rates strictly symmetrically in an environment of increased divergences in economic growth. In Chart 4.4 I show annual M3 growth and short-term interest rates. As can easily be seen, the ECB conducted its interest rate policy largely without taking cues from M3 growth. Rates edged higher in 1999–2000 although M3 growth eased, and rates came down in 2001–5 while M3 growth accelerated. The ECB reacted late to the acceleration of money growth as of mid-2004 with a rate hike in December 2005. It again reacted late to the sharp drop in money growth in the autumn of 2007, with rate cuts after the collapse of Lehman Brothers in September 2008.

As was pointed out by numerous academics and financial market economists after the first few years of interest rate policy, decisions could be much better explained by the so-called 'Taylor Rule', which relates the interest rate policy of the central bank to the evolution of inflation against the central bank's target and the output gap (i.e., the percentage difference between actual GDP and potential GDP) of the economy. This is illustrated in Chart 4.5 where I plot a series of three-month interest rates based on this rule, giving equal weight to the inflation and output gaps and using the 1999–2007 average of short-term rates as the neutral rate, and the actual ECB refinancing (refi) rate. By and large, the rule explains the ECB's interest rate policy rather well.

However, the rule-based series is much closer to the actual policy rate of the ECB when we use German data for the output gap and the inflation rate for its calculation. This is shown in Chart 4.6. At the beginning of EMU, the ECB's policy rate was perhaps a notch too tight for Germany, but it was much better aligned with economic conditions in Germany in 2002–2010 than with conditions in the euro area at large. Since then, the policy rate has been substantially below the theoretical rate calculated with German data.

As explained earlier, through most of the first decade of EMU, Germany was the 'caboose' in the train of EMU economies in terms of growth. Hence, when the interest rate policy of the ECB was broadly right for Germany, it was probably too easy for most of the other countries, which had either faster growth or higher inflation. Charts 4.7–4.9 show that this was indeed so. In France it was mainly higher growth, in Italy higher inflation and in Spain higher growth and inflation that were responsible for the higher theoretical rates.

By paying relatively little attention to money growth and setting policy rates broadly consistent with the Taylor Rule,

Chart 4.7. France: Taylor rate vs. ECB main refi rate

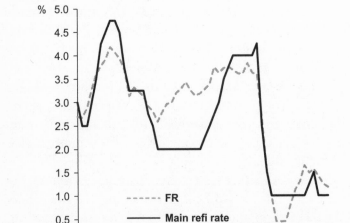

Source: Deutsche Bank Research

Chart 4.8. Italy: Taylor rate vs. ECB main refi rate

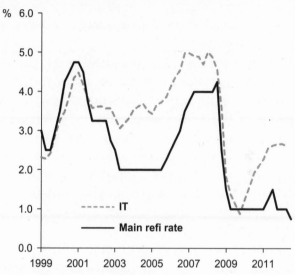

Source: Deutsche Bank Research

Chart 4.9. Spain: Taylor rate vs. ECB main refi rate

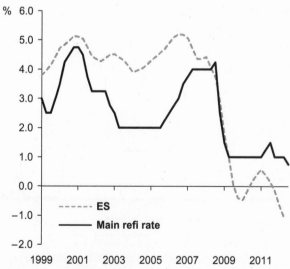

Source: Deutsche Bank Research

the ECB's monetary policy in effect came fairly close to the
policy of inflation targeting that is pursued by many other
central banks. A key element in this strategy is to keep the
utilization of economic capacity at a level consistent with
stable inflation (i.e., to avoid under- or overutilization of
capacity as indicated by a negative or positive output gap).
As my colleague Mike Biggs from Deutsche Bank and I have
argued, such a strategy is entirely blind to developments in
the credit markets and may inadvertently contribute to the
formation of credit and asset price bubbles.[3] As illustrated
in Chart 4.10, this seems to have happened in the euro area
during the 1990s and 2000s. Estimated output gaps were
closely correlated with credit growth, and an output gap of
zero (i.e., a capacity utilisation apparently consistent with
stable inflation) went along with nominal credit growth of
7.0 per cent. With nominal GDP growth of less than

Chart 4.10. Euro area output gap and credit growth

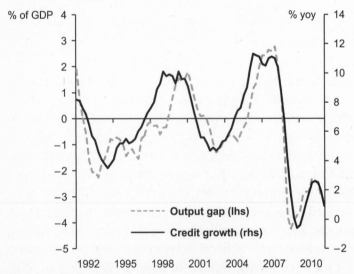

Source: OECD, ECB, Deutsche Bank Research

4 per cent, the ratio of credit to GDP could rise to unsustainable levels without triggering any alarm bells.

By giving less weight to money and credit growth than to economic activity data and prices in general, and more weight to German activity and price data than would be consistent with the share of the German economy in euro area GDP, the ECB at least indirectly helped to fuel excessive house price increases in a number of countries. Of course, inappropriate effects of monetary policy at the country level could have been offset with country-specific countercyclical provisioning at the national level. Supervisors could have forced banks to step up reserve holdings for credit extended to fund the acquisition of overpriced houses. They could also have limited the ratio of loans to the value of houses and hence cooled the market by requiring buyers to come up with more equity. However, with the exception of Spain, where regulation of this sort existed at least in principle, no systematic attempt was made by national central banks or supervisors to lean against the growing house price bubble. To be fair, the Spanish authorities made some effort to counter the excessive overheating of the real estate market, but they did not prevent the house price bubble and overbuilding. National fiscal policies could also have been used to counter inappropriate country-specific effects of the common monetary policy. But in general this was not the case. Fiscal policy in many countries not only failed to counter a monetary policy that was too soft for domestic economic conditions, but it was often too loose to even satisfy the requirements of the Stability and Growth Pact.

Indeed, black spots in the seemingly bright picture were continuous quarrels about fiscal policy. After having more or less met the fiscal entry criteria for entering into the union, countries tended to soon struggle again with their government budget deficits and only in very few cases succeeded in bringing their elevated debt ratios down to 60 per cent of GDP as promised. Thus, euro area budget balances moved to a small surplus by 2000 but subsequently fell into a deficit of 3.1 per cent of GDP in 2003 and have failed to return to surplus since. The debt ratio eased from 71.5 per cent of GDP in 1999 to 68.2 per cent in 2002 but has increased ever since (see Charts 4.11, 4.12 and Table 4.2 for deficit and debt ratios by country).

It soon became clear that the Stability and Growth Pact lacked the teeth to impose discipline in fiscal policy among EMU members. A key problem was that offending countries were supposed to be judged by their peers, who were mindful that they might also become offenders in the future. The authors of an ECB occasional paper published in 2006 summed up this problem: '...the procedure as laid down in the Treaty is in no sense mechanistic, and ultimately leaves it to the discretion of the EU Council

Chart 4.11. Public deficits in Euroland (per cent of GDP)

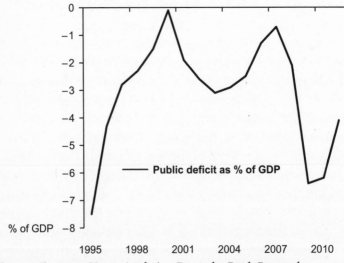

Source: Eurostat, Haver Analytics, Deutsche Bank Research

Chart 4.12. Public debt in Euroland (per cent of GDP)

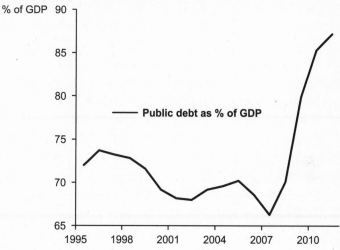

Source: Eurostat, Haver Analytics, Deutsche Bank Research

Table 4.2. Public deficits and debt in key EMU member countries (per cent of GDP)

	Deficits			Debt		
	1999	2007	2011F	1999	2007	2011F
Austria	−2.4	−0.9	−3.2	66.8	60.2	71.2
Belgium	−0.7	−0.3	−3.9	113.6	84.1	96.1
Finland	1.7	5.3	−1.5	45.7	35.2	49.0
France	−1.8	−2.7	−6.0	59.0	64.2	85.4
Germany	−1.6	0.2	−1.3	61.3	65.2	81.7
Greece	−3.1	−6.5	−9.5	100.3	107.4	161.7
Ireland	2.7	0.1	−10.5	48.5	24.8	106.6
Italy	−2.0	−1.6	−4.0	113.7	103.1	120.9
Netherlands	0.4	0.2	−3.5	61.1	45.3	64.2
Portugal	−2.7	−3.1	−6.5	49.6	68.3	105.6
Spain	−1.2	1.9	−6.6	62.4	36.2	69.6

Source: Eurostat, Haver Analytics, DB Global Markets Research

of Ministers of Economic Affairs and Finance...to decide whether to take action.'[4] Hence, despite continual violations of the pact, not a single monetary fine was imposed on any member country during the first ten years of EMU.

A serious blow to the pact's credibility was dealt in November 2003 in the context of an excessive deficit procedure against Germany and France, when it became clear that the measures taken by these countries would not be sufficient to correct their excessive deficits until 2004, as demanded by the council. The European Commission recommended that the council should step up pressure on both countries by issuing 'notices' (the last step before sanctions) and suggested an extension of the deadline to 2005. But the council failed to achieve the 'qualified majority' needed to adopt these decisions. Instead, in view of commitments expressed by Germany and France to take effective action to correct their excessive deficits by 2005, it 'concluded' that the procedures should be held in abeyance. These conclusions were subsequently challenged by the commission and annulled by the European Court of Justice (ECJ) on the grounds that the council had not followed the rules and procedures as set out in the treaty. In particular, the ECJ made clear that the council could not, by itself, take initiatives in the absence of an appropriate recommendation by the commission and could not replace a 'procedure' with political 'conclusions'.[5]

In the event, this episode led to a 'reform' of the pact in March 2005, in which both the 'preventive' as well as the 'corrective' arms of the SGP were made 'more flexible' (i.e., watered down). Specifically, in the preventive arm: (1) instead of having budget balance or surplus as the medium-term budgetary objective, countries could define their own objectives; (2) the adjustment path to the medium-term objective was made more discretionary; and

(3) structural reforms were taken into account as mitigating factors in assessing deficits. In the corrective arm: (1) the definition of a 'severe economic downturn' was defined more clearly as a drop of GDP during a longer period of low growth; (2) a list of 'other relevant factors' was specified to be taken into account in the assessment of deficits; (3) procedural deadlines and deadlines for the correction of excessive deficits were extended; (4) the council was given the right to correct the commission's recommendation when 'unexpected adverse economic events with major unfavourable consequences for government finances' occurred after the adoption of the recommendation or notice; and (5) the focus on debt sustainability was increased.

On 25 March 2005, the ECB issued a statement saying, 'The Governing Council of the ECB is seriously concerned about the proposed changes to the Stability and Growth Pact.' The bank continued, 'It must be avoided that changes in the corrective arm undermine confidence in the fiscal framework of the European Union and the sustainability of public finances in the euro area Member States.' It also added, 'As regards the preventive arm of the Pact, the Governing Council also takes note of some proposed changes which are in line with its possible strengthening.'[6]

The ECB's concerns initially seemed unfounded. Government budget deficits eased from 2.5 per cent of GDP in 2005 to 0.6 per cent in 2007 (Chart 4.11). Until the financial crisis started, only one country (Greece) had government budget deficits continuously in excess of the 3 per cent limit, which at the time was not noticed due to the manipulation of statistics. Government finances in all other countries did not seem alarmingly out of line. In many cases they failed to meet the criteria set at the beginning of EMU and stretched the Stability and Growth Pact, but they did not stand out when compared to other industrial countries. Debt ratios rose sharply only in 2009–11, largely due to the recession but also due in some cases to the recapitalization and takeover of bad debt from commercial banks. This was most pronounced in Ireland and Spain, where debt ratios jumped by 273 per cent and 69 per cent, respectively, between 2007 and 2010.

But if government deficits and debt of EMU member countries were not clearly out of line with those of other industrial countries, why has there been a run from euro area government bonds since 2010? The answer can be found in the inconsistent treatment of the default risk of government debt. As we argued above, the legal framework of EMU implied that government debt was subject to default risk. But neither national authorities nor EU institutions acted as if this were the case. The former failed to reduce their debt below the threshold at which a debtor's default endangers the stability of the financial system. The latter treated euro area sovereign debt as risk-free in financial regulation and collateral requirements for central bank lending. This inconsistency paved the way for an unexpected U-turn in the treatment of Greek public debt from free-of-default risk to subject-to-default risk in July 2011. When the European Council in that month decided to 'volunteer' the private sector to accept a haircut on its claims on the Greek government, financial markets began to consider all sovereign debt in EMU as being subject to default risk. The run from this debt started when it became clear that the ECB was reluctant to act as lender of last resort to systemically important euro area sovereign debtors.

While the performance of government finances during the first decade of EMU was the subject of continuous (albeit fruitless) discussion and admonition at every press conference of ECB presidents, the build-up of large external current account imbalances went almost unnoticed.

Germany and the Netherlands ran large surpluses, the former peaking at 7.4 per cent of GDP in 2007 and the latter at 9.3 per cent of GDP in 2006. Other countries, notably Greece, Portugal and Spain, ran large deficits, peaking at 14.9 per cent of GDP in 2008 in the first case, at 12.6 per cent in the same year in the second case and at 10 per cent in 2007 in the third case. Since the euro area as a whole had a broadly balanced external current account these data largely reflect imbalances within the euro area.

EU officials tended to ignore or downplay concerns about current account imbalances within EMU on the basis that they reflect deeper financial integration made possible by the elimination of exchange rate risk. The commission's comprehensive and detailed report on the euro's first decade, published in May 2008, mentioned current account imbalances among EMU member countries only in passing. It recommended closer monitoring of these imbalances, which could be 'harmful and the result of inefficient adjustment'.[7] Even the ECB, which continuously warned about the dangers emanating from government budget deficits, ignored the dangerous external imbalances. Thus, ECB president Trichet noted in 2006:

Thanks to greater financial integration, economic agents can invest more easily in any part of the euro area and thereby spread the risk of potential local shocks having an impact on income and consumption. The potential benefits of this are very significant. As euro area investors assign more weight to portfolio investment in euro area countries – and banking integration grows as well – risk-sharing in the euro area increases. This is a very important shock absorber.[8]

Table 4.3. Current account balances of key EMU member countries (per cent of GDP)

	1999	2007	2011F
Austria	−1.7	3.5	2.5
Belgium	5.1	1.8	2.5
Finland	5.3	4.3	0.5
France	3.1	−1.0	−2.8
Germany	−1.3	7.4	5.4
Greece	n/a	−14.3	−10.0
Ireland	0.2	−5.3	0.5
Italy	1.0	−1.3	−3.8
Netherlands	3.9	6.7	5.5
Portugal	−8.1	−10.1	−8.0
Spain	−2.9	−10.0	−3.4

Source: Eurostat, Haver Analytics, Deutsche Bank Research

And still, in March of 2008, Trichet felt that 'the fundamentals of the euro area economy remain sound and the euro area economy does not suffer from major economic imbalances'.[9]

These current account imbalances have reflected public and private sector saving–investment imbalances caused by strong growth in private and public consumption as well as housing investment. Wage growth in excess of productivity growth raised unit labour costs and prices in the deficit countries relative to those in the surplus countries (Chart 4.13). All this was made possible by the ready availability of cheap credit against the background of the global credit bubble. As pointed out above, the theory of optimum currency areas suggests that interregional fiscal transfers can be a substitute for labour mobility.

Chart 4.13. Development of unit labour costs since 2000

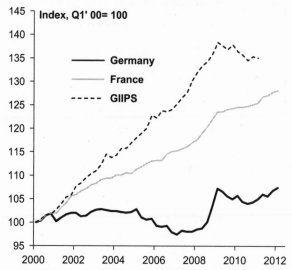

Notes: GIIPS refers to the GDP-weighted average of Greece, Italy, Ireland, Portugal and Spain
Source: Haver Analytics, Deutsche Bank Research

In EMU, where both labour mobility and fiscal transfers are low, cheap credit is substituted for intercountry fiscal transfers, allowing for a convergence of living standards among member countries without large-scale migration or commensurate convergence of production. In other words, cheap credit was the glue that held EMU together during its first decade of existence. Hence, the end of cheap and indiscriminate credit pulled the rug from under EMU. The burst of the global credit bubble forced the ECB and financially stronger countries to step in to avoid the collapse of banks and governments suddenly cut off from market funding. Since none of this was foreseen in its legal framework and no arrangements for crisis management had been made, EMU experienced a crisis of legitimacy. Moreover, as surging risk aversion among private investors left large funding gaps of governments and banks unfilled, EMU experienced a balance-of-payments crisis. These crises are the topics of the next two chapters.

Chapter 5

A Crisis of Legitimacy

'It will not be so that the South cashes in from the so-called rich countries. This would break Europe.'

'And how should this be prevented?'

'With the Treaty of Maastricht and possibly its further development at the proposed Inter-governmental Conference in 1996. There is a "no bail out rule". That means that if a country incurs high deficits through its own action, then neither the Community nor a member state is obliged to help this country.'

'But you cannot let this country default.'

'Why not?'

—Horst Köhler, former German deputy finance minister, managing director of the IMF and president of the Federal Republic of Germany, in an interview with *Der Spiegel* in 1992[1]

The faulty legal framework of EMU and the lack of agreed crisis management procedures forced governments and the ECB to circumvent essential rules on which EMU was based in order to prevent the financial crisis from becoming a disaster. This called the legitimacy of government and central bank actions into question. It all seemed to begin harmlessly with swift liquidity support by the ECB for a gummed-up money market in August 2007. The ECB's unusual action was triggered by a scramble for liquidity caused by the news that euro-denominated money market funds had exposure to the US subprime mortgage market (swapped back into euros). Since the funds were unable to sell their subprime mortgage paper to raise cash for withdrawals of deposited funds by investors, they had to close and freeze investor deposits. In shock over this action, interbank lending dried up as banks suspected each other of having similar value-impaired assets on their balance sheet that could jeopardize their solvency. Thanks to the ECB's determined liquidity injection, failures to meet payments due among banks could be avoided. At first, it seemed that the euro area had escaped a larger financial accident caused by financially engineered products and lax regulatory oversight in the US. For some time after this event, ECB president Trichet was fond of referring to the operation as proof that the ECB was capable of doing the right thing in a critical moment. As the reader will recall from Chapter 3, the Eurosystem had agreed on clear procedures in case it was called upon to act as lender of last resort, and these procedures worked smoothly. However, the exit from this role was less well defined. Hence, while the ECB's initial liquidity support was indeed in line with best practice in central banking, the same cannot be said of the subsequent actions.

As time passed and the full scale of the financial crisis became known, financial institutions came under severe global pressure. What initially looked like a liquidity problem turned into a problem of solvency, as it has so often done in the past. Thus, in September 2007, the British savings bank Northern Rock was cut off from market funding and needed government support. As British deposit insurance was badly designed, covering only a part of the deposit and leaving the depositor at risk for the rest, depositors started a run on the bank, the first in the UK since Victorian times. Then, in March 2008, the US investment bank Bear Stearns was cut off from market funding, received a loan from the Federal Reserve and was taken over by JP Morgan Chase & Co. two days later. In September 2008, the financial crisis came to a head when the US investment bank Lehman Brothers announced a huge loss for the third quarter and five days later, on 15 September, had to file for bankruptcy. On the same day Bank of America rescued Merrill Lynch by taking it over, and the insurance company AIG was propped up by the Federal Reserve. To complement rate cuts and liquidity support by the central banks in the wake of these events, governments in the US and Europe had to step in during the following months and recapitalize or wind down insolvent banks. The US was considerably more active. Between 15 September 2008 (the day Lehman Brothers failed) and the end of 2009, more than one hundred and fifty banks were closed by the Federal Deposit Insurance Corporation. The number of bank closures in Europe could be counted on two hands.

The faulty financial architecture of EMU and the lack of agreed procedures in a widespread financial emergency (rather than of a single institution or a small number of institutions) prevented an adequate response by the EU authorities to the risks created by the financial crisis. While euro area governments avoided the worst outcome in the form of a bank run (like in the UK) or a chaotic collapse (like that of Lehman Brothers in the US) by dealing with the weakest institutions, they operated at national levels and in the event failed to inject sufficient equity into the banking system to return all surviving institutions to robust financial health. As a result, while banks elsewhere

Chart 5.1. ECB long-term refinancing operations with euro area banks

Source: ECB, Haver Analytics, Deutsche Bank Research

were slowly nursed back to health, a significant number of weak banks in the euro area – for which the name 'addicted banks' was coined – remained cut off from market funding and hence dependent on ECB support for the financing of their assets. Long-term lending to banks by the ECB turned into a partial, and for some banks complete, substitute for market funding (see Chart 5.1). Since the ECB was not able to force the governments to recapitalize or close the addicted banks and a number of governments lacked the financial means to do so, they were drawn into the open-ended support of financial institutions that were in danger of turning from being illiquid to being insolvent.

Conditions worsened when market funding for highly indebted countries began to dry up towards the end of 2009. The subprime mortgage crisis in the US started when investors lost trust in debt instruments they had bought on the assumption that they were of the highest quality. In the wake of this event, the loss of trust spread to other instruments and eventually affected a large number of private sector financial institutions. In a similar development, the loss of trust in euro area government debt instruments was started in September 2009 by the disclosure of the newly elected Greek government that its predecessor had lied about the true state of government finances. Instead of the previously estimated 6.7 per cent of GDP, the new government predicted a deficit of 12.7 per cent for 2009 – it eventually reached 15.8 per cent.

To add insult to injury, it subsequently emerged that government finance statistics had been systematically misreported by the outgoing conservative government in a continuation of the practice of its socialist predecessor. Thus, Greece had not only entered EMU on the basis of fraudulent government statistics but continued to report false numbers through most of the years 2001–2009, irrespective of whether the left-wing PASOK party or the right-wing New Democracy party was in power. Despite their seemingly stark ideological differences, the Greek political parties seemed to be united in their lenient approach to disclosing the true state of government affairs to EU authorities. To be fair, the latter also refrained from asking any uncomfortable questions. Since the mid-1990s – the starting point of a new series of Greek government statistics put together by Eurostat, the statistics office of the European Community – Greece never had a deficit of less than 3 per cent of GDP, hence never met this entry criterion for EMU and never complied with the requirements of the Stability and Growth Pact. Moreover, Greece's public debt ratio never came even close to the 60 per cent limit set by the Maastricht Treaty and the

Stability and Growth Pact, but instead moved between 94 per cent in 1999 and 129.3 per cent in 2009 before moving sharply higher thereafter.

The blatant and persistent misreporting of official statistics by the Greek authorities, the tolerance of this behaviour by the EU authorities and Greece's EMU partners and the truly awful state in which Greece's government finances were eventually revealed to be turned into a shock for euro area government debt markets, similar to the blow dealt to private debt markets by the collapse of the subprime segment of the US mortgage market. In both cases, investors felt seriously misled and lost trust in all but the safest debtors. Thus, just as the subprime mortgage collapse in the US marked the beginning of the private sector debt crisis in 2007, the Greek government finance debacle marked the start of the government debt crisis in 2009. Given the weaknesses in the financial architecture of EMU, which are reminiscent of those of the gold standard of the early 1930s, it is not surprising that the government debt crisis triggered by Greece turned into a euro crisis. The catalyst for this was the banking sector.

Traditionally, government debt has been classified as 'risk free' and hence has been exempted from regulatory credit limits or requirements to set aside equity as risk buffer. This practice did not change in EMU, although the Maastricht Treaty allowed for the possibility of sovereign defaults. As a result, banks did not change their habit of holding large amounts of national government bonds on their balance sheets when EMU began. Hence, banks of countries considered credit risks by the capital markets turned into credit risks themselves and were cut off from market funding. To survive, they had to turn to the ECB and became collectively 'addicted' to ECB funding.[2] As a result, the ECB found itself no longer sustaining just individual banks but entire 'banking systems'.[3] Given the governments' weak finances and the absence of a commonly funded and hence credible European deposit insurance and bank resolution regime, the ECB could only end their support of these banks at the cost of a collective failure.

Unable to roll over expiring debt and threatened by bankruptcy, the Greek government in April 2010 received a total of EUR 110 billion in financial assistance from EMU member states (EUR 80 billion) and the IMF (EUR 30 billion) under an adjustment programme expected to run from 2010 to early 2013 and to be managed jointly by the IMF, the ECB and the EU. However, instead of calming the situation, the emergency support for Greece immediately led to fears of bankruptcy of a number of EMU states and a collapse of the euro. Hence, in May 2010, only shortly after the launch of the Greek programme, EMU member governments decided on the creation of a EUR 750 billion support fund for states cut off from market funding (with EUR 60 billion coming from the existing European balance-of-payments assistance facility now dubbed European Financial Stability Mechanism (EFSM), EUR 250 billion from the IMF and EUR 440 billion from a newly created fund dubbed European Financial Stability Facility (EFSF)). Since it took some time to prepare the institutional set-up of this facility, the ECB was enlisted to intervene and stabilize the bond markets of financially troubled countries. As a result, the ECB acquired in the following 12-month period some EUR 75 billion of bonds from Greece as well as from Ireland and Portugal, which eventually also pursued adjustment programmes backed by the EU and IMF. Following a decision by the European Council in July 2011 to force private creditors of Greece to accept a 'haircut' on their bond holdings (equivalent to a

Chart 5.2. The ECB's securities market and covered bond programmes

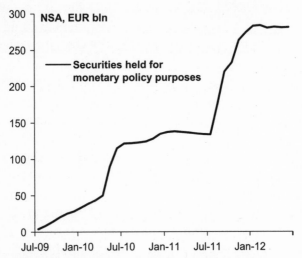

Source: ECB, Haver Analytics, Deutsche Bank Research

loss in the net present value of 21 per cent of their exposure), the Italian and Spanish government bond markets also came under pressure in August 2011. In response, the ECB significantly stepped up its government bond purchases in a programme they now dubbed the Securities Markets Programme (see Chart 5.2 for the ECB's purchases of government and covered bonds for the purpose of easing funding strains by sovereign borrowers and banks).

According to its statutes, the ECB must not buy government bonds in the primary market (i.e., directly from the issuer). This provision was meant to safeguard against central bank funding of government deficits, which after the experience of hyperinflation in 1920s Germany has been anathema to the following generations of Germans. However, like any other modern central bank, the ECB is allowed to buy and sell government bonds (i.e., conduct so-called open market operations) in the secondary market with a view to steering the money supply. Hence, as long as the ECB could justify its bond purchases by appealing to monetary policy, they were not plainly against its statute. Against this background, ECB president Trichet justified the intervention in the government bond markets with the need to restore the monetary transmission mechanism. Owing to the pricing of significant default risk in the bond markets of a number of EMU governments, so the argument went, the monetary policy intentions of the ECB as reflected in short-term interest rates – over which the central bank has a high degree of control – were no longer transmitted to longer duration bonds and hence to borrowing rates for households and companies. By buying longer-duration government bonds, the ECB would flatten excessively steep yield curves in certain countries and consequently ensure that there was no credit crunch for the private sector in these countries.

If one had followed this line of argument one would have needed to believe that the extension of central bank credit to governments implied by the bond purchases was an unintended but unavoidable consequence of a necessary monetary policy strategy. This view was heavily challenged by criticism, mainly coming from Germany. In the view of the critics, the main effect of the ECB's government bond purchase programme was to extend credit to governments cut off from capital markets because of unsound fiscal policies. Restoring the monetary transmission mechanism required an improvement of government finances with a view to reducing risk premiums on the governments' debt. Depressing bond yields through central bank intervention only let these governments off the hook from implementing painful reform by offering central bank funding of deficits and debt as an alternative to market funding. Hence, critics regarded the ECB's purchases of government bonds under its Securities Markets Programme as a violation of Article 123 of the TFEU, forbidding the monetary financing of government debt.

When, in August 2011, the presidents of the ECB and the Bank of Italy linked the purchases of Italian government bonds by the ECB to promises by the Italian government to reduce its fiscal deficit and reform its economy, critics felt that their point had been proven; the ECB's intervention had the character of a fiscal rather than monetary policy measure. Moreover, when Italian prime minister Berlusconi reneged on promises for economic reform given to the ECB leadership, shortly after the ECB intervention had pushed Italian bond yields down by almost 100 basis points, the critics' worst fears about the dangers of linking monetary to fiscal policy had come true. Two German ECB council members, Bundesbank president Weber and ECB executive board member and chief economist Jürgen Stark, felt strongly enough about the legality of this activity that they resigned from their positions in the course of 2010–11.

Not only was the legality of monetary policy actions during the euro crisis questioned. EMU governments, too, were accused of violating Article 125 of the TFEU, forbidding the bailout of financially distressed countries. In Germany, several suits were filed against the financial assistance to Greece and the establishment of the EFSF, which were admitted by the Constitutional Court in the course of 2010–11. While the court, in September 2011, eventually ruled that the financial assistance programmes did not violate the constitutional right of German citizens to exercise democratic control over government finances through the Bundestag and Bundesrat, the court also admonished the government that under the existing constitution there were limits to

the transfer of fiscal sovereignty from the national to the
European level. Most importantly, the court found that it
would be against the constitution if the government or
parliament entered into unlimited automatic financial
obligations towards EU institutions or other EU countries.
Many observers interpreted this ruling as preventing
Germany's participation in the issuance of euro area
government debt under joint and several liability of the
issuers.

Such a pooling of liability for all or a part of governments'
bond issues in so-called eurobonds had been proposed by
numerous EU Commission members, politicians and
commentators as a means to reduce borrowing costs of
governments shunned by the capital markets.[4] It has
been resisted by the German government on the grounds
that it would dilute financial liability, destroy incentives
for prudent fiscal management and raise the costs of
borrowing for Germany. According to Chancellor Merkel,
the introduction of eurobonds could only stand at the end
of a process of more fiscal integration and come after
governments had accepted limits to their sovereignty in
fiscal policy decisions when these decisions had an impact
on other EMU member countries or the entire union.
With this, and in view of the need to change the Basic Law
within the German constitution so as to allow Germany
the assumption of joint liability for European sovereign
debt, the introduction of eurobonds appeared to have been
shifted into the indefinite future. Perhaps in recognition
of these immense hurdles, French president Sarkozy,
after an initially more positive stance, eventually adopted
Merkel's view in opposition to the European Commission
under its president Barroso, which in late 2011 published
a Green Paper on the possible introduction of these
instruments.[5] However, following his election to president

of France, François Hollande started a new push for debt issuance under joint and several liability. As economic conditions deteriorated and access to financial markets became more difficult, the new prime ministers of Italy and Spain, Mario Monti and Mariano Rajoy, joined in the call for eurobonds. In Germany, the main opposition parties, the SPD and the Greens, endorsed the proposal of a European Debt Redemption Fund (EDRF), put forward by the government's Council of Economic Experts in its 2011 annual report. The EDRF is supposed to take over countries' debt in excess of 60 per cent of GDP and fund it through joint bond issuance against commitments (supposedly binding but in reality hardly enforceable) by participating countries to keep their budgets balanced over the cycle, allocate special tax revenue to paying off debt in the EDRF over time and pledge any remaining national gold and foreign exchange reserves as security to the fund.

In the eyes of the critics, the two key pillars on which EMU was built – the central bank's exclusive focus on the purchasing power of the common money and governments' full liability for their financial decisions – had been destroyed by the way the euro crisis had been managed. Especially in Germany, but also in some other northern EMU countries such as the Netherlands and Finland, trust in the EU treaties and pacts was undermined. In the autumn of 2011, this induced Chancellor Merkel to push for a revision of the treaty and for balanced budget amendments in national constitutions, with a view to making commitments to fiscal discipline more binding and legally enforceable by national courts and the European Court of Justice. The criticism and loss of trust could probably have been avoided had emergency procedures been clearly defined for times of financial crises and incorporated into EMU's legal framework. Without such clearly defined procedures, the controversial reading of the actions of EMU governments and the ECB eventually undermined trust in EMU and made an effective resolution of the crisis more difficult.

Chapter 6

A (Hidden) Balance-of-Payments Crisis

'The uneven distribution of central bank liquidity within the Eurosystem provides stability, as it allows financially sound banks – even those in countries under stress – to cover their liquidity needs, thereby contributing to the effective transmission of the ECB's interest rate decisions to the wider euro area economy, with a view to maintaining price stability in the euro area over the medium term.'

—ECB *Monthly Bulletin*, October 2011[1]

If cheap credit was needed for EMU to survive its first ten years, why did it not collapse immediately after the burst of the credit bubble in 2007–8? As the reader will have concluded on the basis of our discussion so far, the answer is that cheap credit from the private capital market was replaced by credit from official sources. To a limited extent, official credit came from other governments or EU institutions. Far more and cheaper credit came from the Eurosystem of central banks. Generous liquidity provision by the ECB (through fixed rate, full allocation refinancing operations with maturities of up to three years) allowed banks cut off from market funding to obtain central bank money from the ECB to fund their outgoing net payments. When entire countries and their banking sectors are cut off from market funding of their net imports of goods and services and of their capital exports, ECB credit is used to fund the resulting balance-of-payments deficit. Banks turn the 'inside money' obtained from the ECB into 'outside money', which then flows via the interbank payment system TARGET2 (Trans-European Automated Real-time Gross settlement Express Transfer system, where the '2' stands for the system upgraded in November 2007) to the countries with balance-of-payments surpluses.

The TARGET system was created to link the existing national interbank payment systems into an EMU-wide system. Cross-border payments among euro area commercial banks are routed through their respective national central banks, with the ECB acting as a clearing house. There are few banks operating across the entire euro area. Hence, banks have tended not to lend to companies or private households in other countries but to the banks of these countries. Therefore, most cross-border payments are payments between different banks that go through the TARGET system. Positions of the national central banks vis-à-vis the ECB in this system can be used to assess imbalances in the balance-of-payments among EMU member countries. Eurosystem central banks in countries with deficits in their TARGET accounts, and hence countries with balance-of-payments deficits, incur liabilities towards the ECB when they make the payments abroad; central banks in the surplus countries accumulate credits towards the ECB when they receive these payments. Imbalances in the TARGET system reflect a situation equivalent to a fixed exchange rate system with misaligned exchange rates, where the central bank of the surplus country with the undervalued exchange rate accumulates foreign exchange reserves from the central bank in the deficit country with the overvalued exchange rate. However, in contrast to the textbook case, where the central bank in the deficit country loses foreign exchange reserves to fund the payment deficits, Eurosystem central banks in deficit countries create central bank money and lend it to the banks in their countries to fund the deficit in the balance-of-payments. Thus, the Eurosystem offers balance-of-payments funding at a very low interest rate, in virtually unlimited amounts, without any conditionality. In this chapter we take a closer look at how this payment system works.

Let's consider the case of a Greek resident, who we call Alexis, buying a German car. After a long wait Alexis finally gets a letter telling him that the car is ready for delivery. He decides to travel to Germany and pick up the car at the factory to save transportation costs and have a holiday at the same time. The sales people of the car company tell him that he is most welcome to pick up the car and enjoy a tour of the factory, provided that the money for the purchase of the car has arrived at the company's account with a major German bank. Alexis therefore instructs Omega Bank in Greece to transfer EUR 60,000 from his account to the account of the car company at Deutschland Bank in Germany. The interested reader can follow the accounting mechanics of these transactions in the textbox below. On receiving the instruction, Omega Bank debits Alexis' account with EUR 60,000 and instructs the Central Bank of Greece to debit its own account there with EUR 60,000 and send the money to Deutschland Bank to the account of the car company. The Central Bank of Greece instructs the ECB to debit its TARGET account with EUR 60,000 and credit the German Bundesbank's account with this amount (see the liabilities and claims of the two central banks towards the Eurosystem in section 2 of the textbox). The Bundesbank, seeing the purpose of the payment on the instruction, credits the account Deutschland Bank holds with it, and the latter in turn puts the money into the account of the car company. Deutschland Bank now has a cash surplus of EUR 60,000, while Omega Bank has a cash deficit of the same amount (reflected in section 2 of the textbox by an increase in liabilities of the Greek bank to the Central Bank of Greece, and an increase in central bank liquidity of the German bank, by EUR 60,000 each). Under normal circumstances, Deutschland Bank would now lend the EUR 60,000 to Omega Bank, and the above described money transfer would occur in the reverse direction. When the Bundesbank transfers the money to the Central Bank of Greece, the TARGET positions that opened up in the first transaction would be closed again and both central banks would return to a neutral position vis-à-vis the ECB (see section 3 of the textbox).

In the end, the external balance-of-payments of Germany would show a trade account surplus as a result of the export of the car and a capital account deficit due to the transfer of money needed to fund the purchase of the car. The Greek balance-of-payments would mirror the German one, showing a trade account deficit due to the import of the car funded by a capital account surplus created by the import of capital. The balance-of-payments of both countries would be in equilibrium. As I said above, this is the way the system was designed to work and how it works in conventional circumstances. But what if Deutschland Bank did not trust Omega Bank or any other bank in Greece? In this case, Deutschland Bank would not lend the money to Omega Bank but may prefer to put it on its account at the Bundesbank for safekeeping, even forgoing interest income as a result. The TARGET balance of the Bundesbank vis-à-vis the ECB would remain in surplus, while that of the Central Bank of Greece would remain in deficit. Omega Bank would have a funding shortage due to the loss of the deposit of the EUR 60,000 and would have to cut the asset side of its balance sheet by calling in credits over this amount, or borrow the money from the ECB through the Central Bank of Greece.

Note that the ECB and the national central banks only get involved because cross-border payments are between different banks and not within one bank operating in both countries. However, since the launch of EMU there has been very little progress in the integration of the banking industry. Banks have continued to operate primarily in their domestic market and most cross-border payments have been between banks and intermediated by the Eurosystem. As a result, the Eurosystem can offset imbalances in cross-border payment flows between banks. By doing so, of course, it assumes the risks associated with such imbalances, like a clearing house that does not insist on a complete match of outgoing and incoming payments.

Thanks to the ECB's decision taken at the beginning of the financial crisis to lend at a fixed rate, with banks receiving as much funds as they have bid for and against a very wide range of collateral, banks in countries cut off from capital markets can escape pressure to cut their balance sheets and are able to fund balance-of-payments deficits. As a result, the Eurosystem places the burden of correcting the misaligned exchange rate through relative price changes on the countries with the balance-of-payments surpluses. To better understand this point, consider the textbook case of two countries in a fixed exchange rate system. Let's assume that the real exchange

Textbox 6.1. Accounting for cross-border payments in EMU – an example

1. Initial balance sheets of national central banks and commercial banks (in EUR)

Bank of Greece		Bundesbank	
Assets	Liabilities	Assets	Liabilities
50,000 Loans to Omega Bank	50,000 Omega Bank deposits	50,000 Loans to Deutschland Bank	50,000 Deutschland Bankdeposits
0 Claims on Eurosystem	Due to Eurosystem	0 Claims on Eurosystem	Due to Eurosystem

Omega Bank		Deutschland Bank	
Assets	Liabilities	Assets	Liabilities
100,000 Loans	100,000 Deposits	100,000 Loans	100,000 Deposits
50,000 Central bank liquidity	50,000 Due to Bank of Greece	50,000 Central bank liquidity	50,000 Due to Bundesbank

2. Balance sheets after Greek costumer pays EUR 60,000 to German company

Bank of Greece		Bundesbank	
Assets	Liabilities	Assets	Liabilities
110,000 Loans to Omega Bank	50,000 Omega Bank deposits	50,000 Loans to Deutschland Bank	110,000 Deutschland Bankdeposits
0 Claims on Eurosystem	60,000 Due to Eurosystem	60,000 Claims on Eurosystem	0 Due to Eurosystem

Omega Bank		Deutschland Bank	
Assets	Liabilities	Assets	Liabilities
160,000 Loans	100,000 Deposits	100,000 Loans	160,000 Deposits
50,000 Central bank liquidity	110,000 Due to Bank of Greece	110,000 Central bank liquidity	50,000 Due to Bundesbank

3. Balance sheets after German bank lends EUR 60,000 to Greek bank

Bank of Greece		Bundesbank	
Assets	Liabilities	Assets	Liabilities
50,000 Loans to Omega Bank	50,000 Omega Bank deposits	50,000 Loans to Deutschland Bank	50,000 Deutschland Bankdeposits
0 Claims on Eurosystem	0 Due to Eurosystem	0 Claims on Eurosystem	0 Due to Eurosystem

Omega Bank		Deutschland Bank	
Assets	Liabilities	Assets	Liabilities
160,000 Loans	160,000 Deposits	160,000 Loans	160,000 Deposits
50,000 Central bank liquidity	50,000 Due to Bank of Greece	50,000 Central bank liquidity	50,000 Due to Bundesbank

Source: Deutsche Bank Research

rate of country A is overvalued and that this country therefore suffers from a balance-of-payments deficit. The corollary to this is that the real exchange rate of country B is undervalued and that this country runs a balance-of-payments surplus. The need to fund the balance-of-payments deficit reduces the level of foreign exchange reserves of the central bank in country A. As a result, its balance sheet shrinks, forcing it to contract the central bank money stock, which exerts downward pressure on the price level. At the same time, the balance-of-payments surpluses swell the foreign exchange reserves of the central bank of country B, leading to a rise in its balance sheet, its central bank money stock and eventually country B's price level. The rise of prices in B relative to those in A corrects the real exchange rate misalignment and restores balance-of-payments equilibrium. Note that adjustment is symmetric: prices in B rise while prices in A fall.

Compare this simple textbook example now to the presently existing monetary adjustment mechanism provided by the Eurosystem. Countries with overvalued real exchange rates use funds provided by the ECB, instead of foreign exchange reserves, to fund balance-of-payments deficits. Banks in these countries fund their net payments abroad by borrowing from their national central banks virtually as much as they want against a very wide range of collateral (including IOUs under Emergency Lending Assistance) and at very low interest rates. As a result, they are under no pressure to reduce their balance sheet and may even expand it, as it appears attractive to borrow additional funds from the ECB with a view to lending them to their national governments at a profit.

Compared to the textbook example, there is no downward pressure on domestic demand and the domestic price level in the balance-of-payments deficit countries emanating from the monetary adjustment mechanism. The relative price change is engineered through upward pressure on prices in the surplus countries. Funds borrowed from the Eurosystem in the deficit countries flow through the interbank payment system to these countries, expand bank balance sheets there and eventually induce a liquidity-driven expansion of domestic demand and an increase in the price level, which then corrects the real exchange rate misalignment. Thus, adjustment under the exceptional monetary regime in the euro area is asymmetric and engineered through price increases in the surplus countries. It is therefore hardly surprising that the latter have exerted political pressure for fiscal austerity, so as to also put pressure for adjustment on the deficit countries. Political leverage is relatively high when the deficit country is small. But it is low when the deficit country is large. When a large country resists external political pressure for fiscal austerity and wage adjustment, it can rely on the funding of internal and external deficits by the Eurosystem to avert financial collapse of the entire EU (or even the global financial system) resulting from sovereign bankruptcy and large-scale bank failures.

Chart 6.1 shows the regional disaggregation of ECB loans in the form of main and long-term refinancing operations as well as emergency lending assistance since 2006. The line in the chart, plotted against the axis on the right-hand side, gives the percentage share of ECB lending to a group of countries consisting of Greece, Italy, Ireland, Portugal and Spain (GIIPS) in total ECB lending. In 2007, the share of loans going to these countries was less than 20 per cent of the total, below their share in euro area GDP of about 25 per cent. Until the beginning of the euro crisis, large German banks tended to act as money centre banks, borrowing an overproportional share from the ECB and intermediating the central bank money to smaller banks and banks in other countries. However, when the financial crisis started to undermine the trust of banks in each other and led to a decline in interbank lending, banks in the GIIPS countries obtained a rising share of ECB loans to compensate for the loss of credit from banks in other countries. Conditions deteriorated significantly when the euro crisis started in 2009–10 with the funding problems of the Greek government. Access of banks in the GIIPS countries to interbank loans dried up, forcing these banks to rely to an ever-higher degree on the ECB for funding the asset side of their balance sheets. From the middle of 2011 on, banks in these countries received about 80 per cent of all ECB loans.

Chart 6.1. ECB standard refinancing plus emergency lending assistance

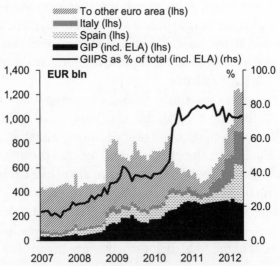

Note: Emergency lending assistance GR 40.1, IE 46.7 EUR bln, latest values

Sources: ECB, NCBs and Deutsche Bank Research

The central bank money obtained by the banks in the GIIPS group, and in other countries with current account deficits that could not be funded with capital account surpluses, was used to fund net payments abroad. This created large increases in TARGET credit and debit positions at the ECB. Most of the payments by the countries with balance-of-payments deficits had to be made to Germany, the country with the largest balance-of-payments surplus among euro area countries. As a result, the claims of the Bundesbank against the ECB under the TARGET system reached EUR 700 billion in the spring of 2012. Chart 6.2 shows the development of ECB loans to the GIIPS countries

Chart 6.2. ECB lending to GIIPS banks and TARGET2 claims of the Bundesbank against the ECB

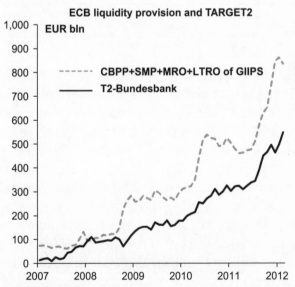

Note: CBPP = covered bond purchase programme; SMP = securities market programme; MRO = main refinancing operations; LTRO = long -term refinancing operations
Sources: ECB and Deutsche Bank Research

Chart 6.3. TARGET2 balances of Germany and GIIPS countries

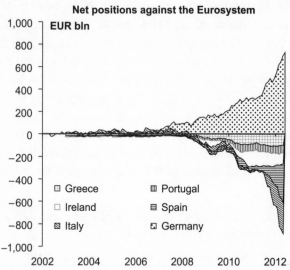

Net positions against the Eurosystem
EUR bln

Legend: Greece, Ireland, Italy, Portugal, Spain, Germany

Sources: Eurostat, Haver Analytics and Deutsche Bank Research

and the associated TARGET balance of the Bundesbank. As time passed, a rising share of net payments from the GIIPS countries went to other euro area countries so that the rise in ECB lending to the GIIPS overtook the increase in the Bundesbank's TARGET position. The development of the distribution of the TARGET positions across euro area countries can be seen in Chart 6.3 and a snapshot of these positions reflecting the state in the middle of 2012 is given in Table 6.1. By that time, the Eurosystem had organized 'loans' through TARGET from the balance-of-payments surplus countries located mostly in the north of the euro area (notably Germany, the Netherlands, Finland and Luxembourg) to the deficit countries (located mostly in the 'Latin' part of the euro area) in the amount of one trillion euros.

Table 6.1. TARGET2 balances (mid-2012, EUR bln)

Germany	728.6
Netherlands	142.5
Luxembourg	124.1
Finland	72.4
AAA countries total	1,067.7
Malta	−1.2
Slovakia	−13.6
Belgium	−31.1
Austria	−37.0
France	−48.2
Portugal	−62.7
Greece	−101.6
Ireland	−102.1
Italy	−274.3
Spain	−408.4

Sources: National central banks and Deutsche Bank Research
Data for Germany, Finland, Belgium, Spain and Italy refer to June 2012; data for the Netherlands, Luxembourg, Malta, Portugal, France, Greece and Ireland refer to May 2012; data for Austria refer to March 2012; and data for Slovakia refer to December 2011

Strictly speaking, of course, the TARGET positions do not reflect loans in the classical sense. As the ECB does not tire to point out, these are accounting positions of the national central banks against the ECB within the Eurosystem created by the 'uneven distribution of liquidity'[2] among euro area banks. However, since euro area banks still predominantly operate in their home country, and most financial transactions between countries are routed through banks and the TARGET system, the positions are a good approximation of the cumulated balance-of-payments positions of euro area countries. Moreover, since the national central banks would end up with these claims and liabilities in the event of a euro break-up, the TARGET positions have at least the character of loans among the euro area countries. These quasi loans arranged through the TARGET system are financial flows entered 'below the line' in the balance-of-payments. 'Above the line' is the current and capital account. When the sum of these two accounts is negative, the balance-of-payments is in deficit. In the case of a single country in a fixed exchange rate system, a balance-of-payments deficit would be funded with a sale of foreign exchange reserves or gold. In the euro area, it is funded through loans from the ECB that give rise to a debit position in the TARGET system. Thus, any official loans extended from the 'northern' to the 'Latin' countries show up in the capital account 'above the line' in the balance-of-payments, and hence come in addition to the quasi loans 'below the line' arranged through TARGET by the Eurosystem.

At the end of the first quarter of 2012, Greece, Ireland and Portugal together had received loan disbursements in the amount of EUR 175 billion from other European countries as part of IMF-led assistance programmes amounting to about EUR 400 billion in total at that time. Of these disbursements, Germany, the Netherlands, Finland and Luxembourg guaranteed EUR 44 billion, a tiny amount compared to one trillion euro of quasi loans from these countries through TARGET. Moreover, the loans under the IMF were extended under strict conditionality to three small countries after agonizing discussions at the technical and political level. The additional trillion in quasi loans was given automatically without any policy conditions to small and large countries in the euro area. Thus, a two-tier support system for troubled EMU countries was created. At the first level, the EU and the IMF extended loans to troubled governments in limited amounts against strict conditionality. At the second level, the ECB extended loans to banks against a wide range of collateral in very large amounts without any conditionality. The two levels were neither coordinated nor connected. Moreover, in a strange distribution of roles, the IMF – originally set up to extend conditional balance-of-payments assistance in the framework of the Bretton Woods system – was enlisted to lead the conditional financial assistance to euro area governments while the ECB engaged in unconditional funding of balance-of-payments imbalances.

Critics of TARGET have argued that the system suffers from a major flaw because national central banks are not required to settle their balances with the ECB on a regular basis.[3] As a result, imbalances can reach levels that in the case of a euro break-up and default of the debtor countries would financially ruin the creditor countries. In the corresponding US interbank payment system Fedwire, which provided the blueprint for TARGET, imbalances among district Federal Reserve banks are settled annually in April by transfers of assets (gold certificates until the early 1990s and US Treasury paper thereafter). The ECB has retorted that there are no limits to payment flows within the currency area formed by the 12 Federal Reserve districts, allowing imbalances in Fedwire positions among the district banks just as in TARGET. The mechanism used to readjust imbalances among districts was only an adjustment key used for the allocation of profits and losses of the US Federal Reserve system to the 12 district reserve banks.[4] But this is exactly the point. The threat of suffering losses induces the reserve banks, in cooperation with the other supervisory authorities (the Federal Deposits Insurance Corporation and federal state governments), to exercise sufficient control over the banks operating in their area so as to discourage them from extending more credit than they can fund in the local market or by attracting funds from other districts. Without such incentives for euro area national central banks, and with unlimited credit allocation from the ECB at low rates against collateral the market would not accept, euro area commercial banks can continue extending credit even when the quality of their assets deprives them of access to market funding. Entire national banking sectors become dependent on the ECB funding their assets when the financial market regards the government debt these banks hold as impaired.

From 2007, the replacement of private sector credit by central bank credit to fund current account imbalances led to a transfer of credit risk from the private to the public sector. If a particular deficit country were to repudiate its debt to the ECB, the losses would be distributed among the remaining EMU members according to their capital share in the ECB (e.g., 27 per cent for Germany). If, however, all deficit countries repudiated their debt (e.g., because of a break-up of EMU), taxpayers in the surplus countries would suffer a loss, possibly amounting to a trillion euro or more. We can only speculate why the designers of the euro area's interbank payment system failed to copy the annual settlement of imbalances from the US Fedwire system. Was it an oversight? Or did countries with traditionally weak external current account balances, in anticipation of future balance-of-payments problems, ensure that they would have unlimited access to the funding of balance-of-payment deficits through the Eurosystem? In any case, the official position with regard to the TARGET imbalances has been that they reflect the temporarily unequal distribution of central bank liquidity across the euro area, which will disappear when trust among banks has been restored. This is undoubtedly correct. But the restoration of trust among banks requires a restoration of trust in the bonds of euro area governments that these banks hold in substantial amounts, and this requires a restoration of trust in the institutional framework of EMU and the correction of unsustainable imbalances among the economies of EMU member countries. Thus, the TARGET imbalances are a reflection of the malfunctioning of EMU and their correction requires no less than the elimination of the faults that have led to the euro crisis.

Meanwhile, as explained earlier, a continuous funding of balance-of-payments deficits of EMU member countries with money created by the ECB would lead to an excess supply of money and eventually raise inflation in the surplus countries (like an excessive accumulation of foreign exchange reserves would do). Thus, surplus countries would see their 'internal exchange rate' appreciate through higher inflation while the price level in deficit countries would be supported by unlimited central bank money supply. Real exchange rate appreciation would set the stage for turning the balance-of-payments surplus into deficit, as more expensive domestic goods would turn net exports into net imports and higher-priced domestic assets would induce the sale of these assets and the purchase of cheaper foreign assets, and hence induce net capital outflows. However, without pressure on deficit countries to deflate their economies, inflation in the surplus countries would have to be quite substantial to achieve the relative price changes necessary to eliminate the balance-of-payments imbalances. In fact, relying on the unlimited downhill money flow from the deficit to the surplus countries to drown the latter in liquidity (so as to generate the necessary relative price changes) could well lead to an uncontrolled rise in inflation in these countries. Excess liquidity tends to accumulate to very high levels before it breaks out into the real economy and asset markets, causing rampant goods and/or asset price inflation. In a fixed exchange rate system, inflation-averse surplus countries would up-value their exchange rate before the accumulation of excess liquidity has made runaway inflation inevitable. In the euro area, such surplus countries would probably need to see runaway inflation before deciding to exit EMU, to be able to let a new currency appreciate and regain control over inflation.

Balance-of-payments imbalances could of course be reversed: the TARGET positions are returned to balance when deficit countries turn their balance-of-payments into surplus by creating a devaluation of their internal real exchange rate through deflation of their goods and asset prices. Net imports of goods and services would turn into net exports, and net capital outflows into net inflows as a result. This could be achieved by tightening the supply of central bank money. Banks in deficit countries would be deprived of funds and would have to shrink their balance sheet by contracting credit. However, enforcing internal real exchange rate devaluation by starving the banking sector of central bank money – so as to create deflation – could lead to a loss of control over the magnitude of deflation, as in the opposite case discussed above, when real appreciation is to be engineered by swamping banks with liquidity. Again, countries that have fallen into uncontrollable deflation could only get out of it again by leaving EMU and radically devaluing their new currency.

To avoid the danger of these extreme outcomes, resulting in a break-up of EMU, the cheap central bank credit could be replaced by fiscal transfers from the surplus to the deficit countries, outright or through joint liability for the public debt (i.e., eurobonds). But this solution would also risk a break-up of the union, as electorates in the surplus countries would most likely resist the use of their taxes to fund deficit countries and probably push for EMU exit. This would seem to leave only one way to redress the unsustainable balance-of-payments imbalances without breaking up EMU like the gold standard of the early 1930s. Supply-side reforms to enhance economic flexibility, so as to allow a reallocation of resources from the nontraded to the traded goods sector, together with a restrictive fiscal policy (with a view to dampening domestic demand and reducing government debt) would be needed to create mild deflationary pressures in the deficit countries. At the same time, a neutral fiscal policy in the surplus countries, coupled with low ECB interest rates for the euro area as a whole, would exert mild inflationary pressures in the surplus countries. The ECB's liquidity policy would need to be generous enough to avoid triggering a deflationary spiral in the deficit countries and restrained enough to exert adjustment pressure on the banks in these countries. Fiscal transfers from the surplus to the deficit countries on a scale that would not exceed taxpayers' tolerance could assist the adjustment process. The optimal policy mix would be achieved when the centrifugal political forces, unleashed by inflation and fiscal transfers in the surplus countries and by deflation in the deficit countries, do not exceed the political will in both country groups to keep EMU together. Of course, achieving and sustaining this policy mix until EMU is again on safe ground is tantamount to the most daring political high wire act, requiring unprecedented political skill in all the relevant decision makers.

Chapter 7

Forward or Backward?

'In principle, I think that there are two economically sustainable approaches to designing a stability-oriented monetary union for the future. The first would be a return to the founding principles of the system agreed in the treaties, which still essentially applies; this would entail having European rules for national fiscal policy, countries retaining their fundamental fiscal policy independence, applying the no bail-out principle and financial markets disciplining fiscal policy. Despite all the comments to the contrary, I still believe that it is possible to successfully stabilise and consolidate this framework. The other approach would be to embark upon a major shift entailing a fundamental change in the federal structure of the EU. This would involve a transfer of national responsibilities, particularly for borrowing and incurring debt, to the EU.'

—Jens Weidmann, president of the Bundesbank, in 2011[1]

In 1991, Bundesbank president Hans Tietmeyer warned that 'a European currency will lead to member-nations transferring their sovereignty over financial and wage policies as well as monetary affairs', and concluded that 'it is an illusion to think that States can hold on to their autonomy over taxation policies'.[2] His warning was echoed in the Bundesbank's Annual Report of 1995, which admonished politicians: 'As a monetary union represents a lasting commitment to integration which encroaches on the core area of national sovereignty, EMU participants must also be prepared to take further steps towards a more comprehensive political union.'[3] Hence, it was only logical that former ECB president Trichet, when he received the 2011 Charlemagne Prize on 2 June in Aachen, proposed the creation of 'a ministry of finance of the Union' that would

> exert direct responsibilities in at least three domains: first, the surveillance of both fiscal policies and competitiveness policies, as well as the direct responsibilities mentioned earlier as regards countries in a 'second stage' [where a country has failed to follow an adjustment programme] inside the euro area; second, all the typical responsibilities of the executive branches as regards the union's integrated financial sector, so as to accompany the full integration of financial services; and third, the representation of the union confederation in international financial institutions.[4]

At the end of 2011, Chancellor Merkel launched a watered-down variant of this grand plan in the form of a new treaty among EMU countries and eight other EU members trying to tie down binding rules for fiscal discipline. The reasoning behind Merkel's initiative is fully in line with the past logic of driving forward European integration through a sequence of steps in the economic and monetary

domain that eventually result in political union, where
key elements of national sovereignty in fiscal policy are
shifted to the supranational level. But is this logic still
valid today?

I believe the answer to this question is no. As I explained
earlier, the 'European method' (the political and business
elites pulling their reluctant citizens along with them as
they drive integration forward) lost its power when the fall
of the Berlin Wall and the peaceful unification of Germany
removed the threat of war from the European region. A
clear signal that the peoples of Europe are not in favour
of a loss of national sovereignty was given in 2005 by the
public rejection of the Lisbon Treaty in France and the
Netherlands, two core European states. The Lisbon Treaty
represented a rather small step towards political union
(and could therefore be implemented nonetheless when
it was stripped of those parts referring to closer political
union). Compared to this, the permanent relinquishment
of budgetary sovereignty would be a major leap forward
and probably rejected in the vast majority of EMU
member states when put to a referendum (or even a vote
in parliament).

It is indeed difficult to see how a full-fledged political
union could work in Europe. Such a union would
encompass joint decisions in key areas of fiscal and
social policy. In the spirit of the principle of subsidiarity,
national and local political bodies would of course remain
responsible for decisions affecting those countries,
regions and local entities. But just as the sovereignty of
local or regional entities is limited by common interest
at the national level, so would national sovereignty in a
European political union be limited by common interest
at the European level. Without such limits, the pursuit of
national economic interests would almost certainly create

negative economic spillover effects among countries and lower economic welfare at the European level. The reckless borrowing of Greece to fund a living standard for its population way beyond its own economic means is a case in point. The de facto bankruptcy of this little country, accounting for no more than 2.5 per cent of euro area GDP, was capable of pushing the EU into the deepest political crisis since its birth. Large-scale fiscal transfers among countries and debt issuance under joint and several liability – measures that a considerable number of observers recommend to overcome the euro crisis – have been put in place for Greece during the last decade. Greece has received annual funds close to 2.5 per cent of its GDP from the EU budget. From 1994 to 1999, about EUR 16 billion in EU structural funds and Greek national financing were spent on projects to modernize and develop Greece's transportation network in time for the Olympics in 2004. The centrepiece was the construction of the new international airport near Athens, which opened in March 2001 soon after the launch of the new Athens subway system. EU transfers to Greece continued, with approximately EUR 19 billion (about 8 per cent of GDP) in structural funds for the period 2000–2006. The same level of EU funding, EUR 19 billion, was allocated for 2007–2013.[5]

Moreover, as financial markets did not believe in the no-bailout clause of the Maastricht Treaty and until the beginning of the euro crisis treated government debt of EMU member countries as if it had been issued under joint liability, Greece enjoyed virtually unlimited access to borrowing at very low cost. Without effective control from the EU level, the transfers and loans were used to finance public and private consumption and construction instead of investments in the production capacity of the country. As Michalis Chrysochoidis, the Greek minister of economics in the Papademos government, put it:

> Over two decades we destroyed our production capacity and industry. In the first decade of this century, after entry into EMU, we could also excessively borrow at low rates, and we did. As a result, we became a country of importers...while we received the money from the EU with one hand we did not invest with the other hand in new and competitive technologies. Everything went into consumption. The result was that those who produced something closed their factories and opened import companies because they could make more money with this.[6]

Clearly, the Greek experience suggests that what some consider the solution to the problem – fiscal transfers and joint liability for sovereign debt – was actually its source. EU authorities claimed that the case of Greece was 'exceptional and unique'. But other countries also overborrowed as long as capital markets generously offered cheap loans, albeit not at the extreme level of Greece. Who can guarantee that such behaviour would not continue and become more widespread if it remains unpunished? The first casualty would be fiscal discipline across the entire monetary union, the next probably price stability when the central bank is enlisted to fund government debt issuance. Hence, to make EMU work, the essence of political union would have to be the surrender of national sovereignty and not fiscal transfers and joint debt issuance.

Chancellor Merkel recognized this when she declared her intention to create a 'fiscal union' consisting of binding rules for fiscal discipline. However, the experience of the first decade of EMU suggests that it is unrealistic to expect sovereign states to abide by strict fiscal policy rules when there is no strong political force at the centre to police those rules, even when they are laid down in international treaties. What is needed is a European public sharing common principles and ideas that are articulated in the European Parliament, executed by a European government and trickle from there to lower levels of government at the national and regional level. But in view of the considerable differences in culture and language barriers, how could political parties and candidates for political office formulate and present programmes for the whole of Europe that would form European government policy and guide fiscal policy at the lower levels of government? How could a common political discussion be organized? Would a European Parliament with members elected mainly on the basis of their nationality have the democratic legitimacy to elect a European government and decide on legislation affecting people's daily lives? It is of course conceivable that, in the absence of commonly developed and shared principles to guide policy at all levels, one country could assume the role of the dominant power and impose common principles on the rest. But if a European political union would be created in such an authoritarian way, it almost certainly would soon be torn apart again by political movements for secession in the smaller countries which would find their national interests oppressed by the dominating power. 'As a young man I always fought for the United States of Europe', says Martin Schulz, the president of the European Parliament. 'Today I know that this won't happen.'[7]

If a leap forward to a much closer political union is against the wish of the peoples of Europe, EMU can only be stabilized when we go back to its key building principles of a common currency shielded from political influence and the full liability of sovereign decisions taken at the national level. This would require that the ECB refrain from lending to banks and states that may be insolvent and returns to its main task of preserving the purchasing power of money. It would also require that the principle of member states' full financial liability is restored, even when this requires allowing them to default on their debt, whereby the external effects of such a default would have to be contained along the lines extensively discussed since the outbreak of the Greek crisis (see below). Above all, it would require that the economies of EMU member countries be made fit to live with a hard budget constraint.

The budget constraint of a country in its broadest form is given by the sum of its capital market borrowing capacity and the seigniorage derived from issuing non-interest-bearing central bank money to banks and the general public. Seigniorage rises when inflation accelerates. Hence, in a 'hard currency regime', the government must refrain from extending its budget constraint by boosting seigniorage through inflation. But this is only possible when the economy is flexible enough to adjust to the government's capital market borrowing capacity without default. For deficit countries to restore their borrowing capacity in the new environment of tight credit measures to reduce public debt levels, it is essential to regain international competitiveness and improve growth prospects. The role model for these countries could be the United States of the nineteenth century, in which the principle of fiscal responsibility was established by the Senate's rejection of requests from federal states for a financial bailout in 1842. The US political regime of that time combined sovereignty at the state level with fiscal responsibility in a community of equals and seems a more promising model for Europe than, for instance, having Germany play the role of the dominating power that enforces fiscal discipline through political pressure. The challenge is to move away from the present unstable state of affairs where economies lack the flexibility to function smoothly in a monetary union and governments are so heavily indebted that they represent a danger to the entire euro area. During the transition, both pressure and help for adjustment are required.

Pressure for adjustment can be created through supervision of national economic and fiscal policies by community institutions and peers and the threat of sovereign bankruptcy, with the consequence of being cut off from capital market funding for an indefinite period of time. Of course, in the case of large countries such as Italy or Spain, the threat of bankruptcy may not be credible. The fallout of the complete default of these countries for global financial markets would be intolerably high. But the fallout can be contained if losses to investors are limited through insurance. For instance, EMU member countries could commit themselves to assume joint liability for the debt of each other in case of default, up to a limit equivalent to 60 per cent of GDP of the country. This limit has been used frequently in EU treaties as the threshold for the long-term sustainability of debt burdens. Insurance of this type is similar to insurance for a catastrophic loss, where the insured bears the first part of any loss but is protected from total loss.

It is different from the 'first loss insurance' provided by the EFSF, where investors would be compensated for the first, relatively small part by the insurance and left to bear the remaining part up to a total loss themselves.[8] It also differs from the idea of issuing debt in two tranches, where the senior tranche is guaranteed by all EMU member states and the junior tranche is only backed by the credit of the individual countries.[9] The 'second loss insurance' sketched here would only pay in case of default and reduce the risk that default would turn into a financial catastrophe. Since it allows investors to estimate their expected maximum loss in case of default (given by the uninsured, first part of a country's debt exceeding 60 per cent of its GDP multiplied with the probability that a default occurs), second loss insurance could also help to establish spreads among EMU government bond yields, reflecting a more rational assessment of the creditworthiness of a country than in the case where recovery values after default are left unclear. Insurance of the sort discussed here would also avoid a moral hazard in borrowing that occurs when all debt is issued under joint liability. Last but not least, catastrophe insurance would not be against the no-bailout principle for overindebted countries or careless investors. Both borrowers and lenders would have to bear costs, the former in the form of losing access to capital markets and the latter in the form of a financial loss, but the costs would be contained so as to avoid a failure of the entire financial system.

Help for adjustment can be provided by an institution responsible for the monitoring of economic policies, identification of adjustment needs and conditional financing when imbalances have led to a sudden stop in market financing. In the extreme case when a country has run up so much debt that repayment is beyond its capacity to generate the resources for debt service, this institution would also organize an orderly debt restructuring with as few external effects on other debtors as possible. What I sketch here is of course nothing other than an IMF for Europe, or a European Monetary Fund (EMF).[10] As we discussed in Chapter 3, Keynes and White conceived such an institution for the Bretton Woods system of quasi-fixed exchange rates against the background of the failures of the gold standard in the early 1930s, when the absence of adjustment funding had led to a global financial crisis. In view of this experience, it is indeed amazing that the fathers of EMU omitted the creation of an equivalent institution for EMU. The EMF could exert the necessary pressure for adjustment through the monitoring of economic developments. It could also give help for adjustment through temporary financing in case of liquidity crunches and make debt restructuring possible by implementing the insurance scheme described above and, as a measure of last resort, arranging debt swaps in return for partial debt forgiveness. I shall come back to the design of this institution in more detail in Chapter 10, when we discuss a potential new architecture for EMU.

As policymakers have responded to the evolving euro crisis, they have taken measures that go in the direction indicated above, but in a number of respects still fall short of what is required for the recreation of a stable base for EMU. Thus, EU leaders have created a rudimentary EMF in the form of the EFSF, launched economic adjustment programmes for Greece, Ireland and Portugal, and in the case of Greece, when insolvency of the government could no longer be denied, organized a debt exchange combined with debt forgiveness. Moreover, at their summit in December 2011, EU leaders set out to harden countries' budget constraints through an intergovernmental treaty establishing legally binding rules for fiscal policy: the treaty on stability, coordination and governance (SCG Treaty) in the EMU. The signatories of this treaty commit themselves to keep their budgets in balance or surplus so that their structural deficit does not exceed 0.5 per cent of GDP, except under extraordinary circumstances beyond their control. This rule is to be reinforced by its incorporation into national law, preferably into the constitution. Mechanisms are to be put in place to ensure timely correction of any deviations from the rule. When the debt-to-GDP ratio exceeds 60 per cent, governments are to reduce it at an average rate of one twentieth per year. For example, if the actual debt ratio is 120 per cent, governments must ensure that it declines by three percentage points ((120–60) / 20) per year. When the European Commission or a signatory state of the treaty concludes that there has been a violation of the treaty, one or more signatory states can launch a suit against the violator at the European Court of Justice.

In parallel, EU leaders agreed to launch the European Stability Mechanism (ESM) in mid-2012 to eventually succeed the EFSF, which expires in mid-2013. Like the EFSF, the ESM can lend to countries to fund adjustment programmes (run by the IMF, the commission and the ECB), give 'precautionary financial assistance' to countries in the form of a credit line, help in recapitalizing banks in EMU member countries and intervene in the primary and secondary government bond markets. Unlike the EFSF, the ESM is to be capitalized with EUR 700 billion, of which EUR 80 billion will be paid in by countries based on their share in the capital of the ECB; the rest will be callable when needed. This is supposed to give the institution a lending capacity of EUR 500 billion (the same as the EFSF and EFSM combined). The ESM has the status of 'preferred creditor', meaning that it is senior to all private creditors and junior only to the IMF. Moreover, 'In accordance with IMF practice, in exceptional cases an adequate and proportionate form of private sector involvement shall be considered in cases where stability support is provided accompanied by conditionality in the form of a macro-economic adjustment programme.'[11] In other words, the ESM can arrange a debt restructuring on a case-by-case basis when this is needed to restore a country to solvency.

To facilitate debt restructuring when needed, all euro area government bonds will be issued with collective action clauses as of 2013.

Clearly, the SCG and ESM treaties go a long way in repairing the severe shortcomings of the original EMU architecture. But they also leave a number of important questions open. Why should we expect countries to now subordinate their budgetary sovereignty under another international treaty and accept enforcement by the European Court when they blatantly breached the Maastricht Treaty and the Stability and Growth Pact? Who will act as a lender of last resort to governments when capital markets have dried up even for the ESM? So far during the crisis, the ECB has helped the banks very generously (and thereby funded the balance-of-payments deficits of a number of countries), but rejected the role of lender of last resort for governments. But is this aversion justified and can it be sustained? We shall discuss these and related questions in the following two chapters.

Chapter 8

In Search of a Lender of Last Resort

'Stressing the role of the central bank as the ultimate buyer of public debt should be seen as an indication of the pathological state of public finances, not as a sign of strength.'

—Otmar Issing, former chief economist of the ECB, in the *Financial Times*, 2011[1]

Since the days of Walter Bagehot, the role of the central bank as a lender of last resort to the banking sector in times of liquidity logjams has been well established. In the course of the financial crisis and the euro crisis, the ECB has not hesitated to assume this role. In fact, the ECB has gone far beyond Bagehot's advice to 'lend freely but at a penalty rate' and lent at low rates even to banks whose solvency was in doubt. But the ECB has refused to act as a lender of last resort to governments and instead justified its government bond purchases with the aim of oiling the monetary transmission mechanism. As in the case of Italy, where bonds were purchased in August 2011 in return for promises of fiscal adjustment (which were not kept), the ECB's explanation sounded a bit hollow and created the impression that the ECB was unable to follow its own principles. Indeed, the ECB's official rejection of the role of lender of last resort to illiquid sovereign debtors recalls the troubles under the gold standard of the early 1930s. As we discussed in Chapter 3, the absence of a lender of last resort to Germany, which had benefited from hot money inflows during the 'roaring twenties' and was suddenly cut off from funding after the stock market crash of 1929, caused widespread bank failures in 1931 and pushed the economies of the Western world into the Great Depression.

Obviously, because of its eminent importance for banks, the default of a sovereign debtor can create as much as or even greater damage to the financial system than a systemically important financial institution. But who else than a central bank, with its ability to create money out of nothing, can act as lender of last resort at the height of a financial crisis? On the other hand, governments may abuse access to central bank credit. The most drastic example of this in modern history is the disastrous monetization of government debt by the German Reichsbank in the early 1920s. The hyperinflation of 1923, resulting from the money printing of the Reichsbank, rewarded debtors and impoverished the middle class.[2] Some historians trace the failure of the Weimar Republic and the rise of the Nazi Party to the economic consequences of hyperinflation. Mindful of the post–World War I historical experience, Otmar Issing, the ECB's first chief economist, has strongly rejected the role of a lender of last resort for the ECB:

Pressing the ECB into the role of ultimate buyer of public debt of individual member states would create the biggest conceivable moral hazard. On top of these alarming economic and monetary consequences, providing monetary financing would break the law – a constitution ratified by all governments and parliaments.[3]

Clearly, the risk of moral hazard that arises when a systemically important debtor – a bank or a government – receives liquidity support from the central bank must not be taken lightly. Bagehot took it seriously enough to call for lending at a penalty rate and against good collateral. But rejecting the central bank's function as lender of last resort for governments but allowing it for banks is logically inconsistent and represents the inverse of a 'category mistake' (where attributes of two different things are compared as if they were of the same nature). Both may be systemically important debtors and both may succumb to moral hazard when they receive liquidity support from the central bank. Hence, on the basis of this argument, the central bank should be lender of last resort to neither. But is the central bank not indirectly playing the role of lender of last resort to governments when it lends to banks that have lent to governments? This would be true if banks were the only sources of government borrowing. In reality, however, governments borrow mostly in the capital markets and banks fund only part of the governments' debt by purchasing government bonds for their own investment account. This leaves us with the conclusion that in a financial system where credit is extended through both banks and capital markets, a central bank ought to act as a lender of last resort to all systemically important debtors, be they banks or other entities fitting into this category.

To better understand the role of a lender of last resort, it helps to turn to David Graeber's history of debt and money, as referred to in previous chapters. Graeber provides historical evidence that economic exchange among individuals in ancient societies initially occurred by giving credit and incurring debt based on trust. Only when there was no trust, as happened when a society entered into an exchange with a foreign one, exchange occurred through trade, which was eventually facilitated by the use of money. More recently, credit was not extended on the basis of trust among individuals but on the belief that credit risks could be accurately measured and minimized with modern techniques of portfolio diversification. This belief paved the way for a big increase of credit extension on a global scale. The role of money as a means of exchange paled in comparison to its role as a measure of credit and debt. According to OECD statistics, the stock of narrow money (M1), consisting of cash and sight deposits generally used for monetary payments in transactions, increased little more than eightfold between the first quarter of 1981 and the third quarter of 2011. By contrast, according to BIS statistics, the stock of outstanding international debt securities (a measure of credit) increased thirty-three-fold during the same period.

However, when unexpected defaults in 2007 of structured mortgage instruments in the US revealed flaws in the models used by rating agencies and banks to assess credit risk, trust in private capital market institutions began to disappear and private credit temporarily collapsed towards the end of 2008. Similarly, when the Greek authorities were found at the end of 2009 to have lied to their lenders about the true state of their finances and the Italian authorities were perceived in July 2011 to have taken their obligation for debt service rather lightly, trust in euro area sovereign debt was lost and a run from EMU government bonds began.

When debt can no longer be refinanced it needs to be settled in legal (or commonly accepted) tender or else the debtor defaults. When the debtor is insolvent, supplying him with legal tender so that he can settle his debt devalues the legal tender received by the creditor by an amount equivalent to the bad debt. In real terms, the creditor is no better off than if the debtor had defaulted, although money illusion may soften the blow. But when the debtor is only illiquid and not insolvent, due to a panic in financial markets that has destroyed all trust among creditors and debtors, supplying him with legal tender to settle his debt prevents an unnecessary and harmful default. In the midst of a financial crisis, when markets are closed for the issuance of new debt even for debtors with the best credentials, the supply of legal tender can only come from the central bank. Whether a central bank lends to banks or other systemically important debtors (such as governments), its dilemma is the same: when it lends to an insolvent debtor it devalues the money it creates; when it lends to an illiquid debtor it prevents unnecessary defaults. When the central bank is unable or unwilling to increase the supply of money, as was the case in the early 1930s, almost all transactions based on credit will freeze, causing what the economist Irving Fischer at the time called 'debt deflation'.

In view of the risks associated with assuming the role of lender of last resort, the central bank ought to perform this role in close cooperation with a fiscal authority. The latter will have to make sure that central bank credit is only given to illiquid financial institutions or governments, and insolvent entities will enter bankruptcy proceedings, in which their debt can be restructured. The IMF was built according to this principle as a lender of last resort to countries with balance-of-payments problems within the post–World War II Bretton Woods system of fixed exchange rates. The IMF is funded by central banks and provides adjustment credits to governments under policy conditionality. Programmes are designed such that a country cut off from capital markets is returned to solvency and its capital markets to liquidity. Against the background of the failings of the gold standard in the early 1930s and the apparent need for an IMF in the Bretton Woods system, it is amazing that an equivalent institution was not built for EMU.

In the summer of 2011 it was suggested to give the EFSF a banking license so as to allow it access to ECB funds in case of an emergency.[4] The idea was to back the EFSF with the unlimited firepower of the ECB so as to make its interventions in the secondary bond market for a large country (e.g., Italy) effective and relieve the ECB from buying bonds in the context of its controversial Securities Markets Programme. Interventions were to be accompanied by conditions for economic adjustment laid out by the IMF, ECB and European Commission (the so-called 'Troika'). Any request for the funding of interventions made by the EFSF would only be fulfilled by the ECB when this was possible without endangering the purchasing power of money in the entire euro area. Thus, all intervention decisions would require the consent of both the Troika and the ECB, and leave the latter firmly in charge of monetary policy and the pursuit of price stability. Although a number of governments – including that of France – supported the idea, the Bundesbank and German government rejected it. At the same time, the German authorities lobbied for preventing the successor of the EFSF, the ESM, from having access to central bank credit in emergencies. The reasoning behind this position was probably similar to that of Otmar Issing discussed above.

During the second half of 2011, government and bank bond markets in the southern part of the euro area began to seize up, pushing yields for both borrowers to unsustainably high levels. Apart from worries about the viability of government finances in a slowing economy, a stress test of banks' balance sheets by the European Banking Authority (which required banks to write down their holdings of euro area sovereign debt to market value and at the same time meet a 9 per cent core Tier 1 capital ratio) added to market nervousness. Against this background, the ECB opted in December for two big liquidity injections into banks in the form of a three-year long-term refinancing operation (LTRO) against a wide range of securities as collateral. Take-up was massive, with a gross allocation of funds of EUR 489 billion in the first tender on 22 December 2011 and another EUR 529.5 billion in the second tender on 29 February 2012. Markets reacted favourably and the yields of beleaguered government bond markets declined. The roller coaster in markets can be inferred from the developments of Italian bond yields shown in Chart 8.1. Yields surged in June–July on the back of worries about the economic and fiscal policies of the Berlusconi government. They came down in August on the back of ECB purchases of Italian government bonds in return for Berlusconi's promises of more fiscal consolidation and economic reform, given to the presidents of the ECB and Bank of Italy. When Berlusconi reneged on these promises a little later, yields rose again, reaching levels of around 7.5 per cent in November. The allocation of large long-term refinancing operations, together with the replacement of the Berlusconi government by a cabinet of respected experts under the leadership of Mario Monti, then helped to ease tensions and bring yields back towards 5 per cent. In the course of 2012, however, yields edged up again when market worries focussed on the state of government finances and the banking sector in Spain, leading to a substantial rise in Spanish government bond yields.

Chart 8.1. ECB action contributing to relief for Italy

Sources: Haver Analytics and Deutsche Bank Research

At first glance, the ECB policy of flooding the banks with liquidity, thus helping the governments through the banks, would seem to show a viable way out of the quarrel over the lender of last resort in EMU and restrict this role of the ECB to banks only. However, funnelling central bank credit through banks to governments raises the risk that adjustment pressure on both governments and banks will be reduced. For governments, the ability to sell their bonds to banks would certainly ease funding tensions in the short term. At the same time, however, it would be subject to the same criticism as the ECB's Securities Markets Programme, namely that central bank funding of government debt relieves governments from implementing economic adjustment programmes. The resulting monetization of government debt would then raise inflation risks for the future. Government funding through commercial banks instead of the ECB would be even more problematic as financing would become available to all governments, irrespective of whether they follow adjustment policies or not. The generous liquidity provision by the ECB also allows banks having difficulties in accessing markets (owing to the perceived low quality of their assets) to maintain or even grow their balance sheet. To the extent that these banks suffer from a liquidity shortage, bridge funding by the central bank is of course appropriate. However, a number of banks, especially in southern European countries, may also need to write off assets, such as mortgages extended for the purchase of houses at inflated prices, and hence require fresh capital either from the market or official sources. Such bank restructuring would be undermined by an overly generous provision of funds from the central bank. Instead of going through painful restructuring, banks may use cheap central bank money to fund large-scale purchases of government bonds in the hope of using profits from the carry trade to strengthen their balance sheets.

Since government bonds do not require equity to be set aside under Basel regulatory rules (i.e., are 'zero-risk-weighted'), balance sheet expansion via the purchase of government bonds does not impair regulatory (i.e., Tier 1 or core Tier 1) capital ratios. In principle, profits from carry trades with government bonds would seem to be an easy way to repair banks' balance sheets and they were used to this effect by Japanese banks in the decade after the burst of the bubble economy in the early 1990s. However, one should be under no illusion that these profits would not represent transfers from the taxpayer, who has to pay the interest on government bonds, to the banks. The latter get central bank money at very low cost and hence deprive the central bank, and in turn the taxpayer, from seigniorage income, which arises from central bank lending at positive interest. Perhaps more worryingly, large acquisitions of home country government bonds ties banks and governments closer together, unwinding earlier developments towards the creation of an integrated euro area financial market, and could damage the real economy. The substitution of lending to companies with lending to governments – which improves the regulatory capital ratios – would create a credit crunch for the private sector and exacerbate an economic downturn already under way in response to inevitable government budget deficit reduction. This would in turn make it more difficult for highly indebted governments to return to the market and start a vicious circle. When government bonds are seen as risky by investors, they regard the banks holding large amounts of these government bonds as risky as well and hence avoid lending to them. Unable to access the market, these banks then become reliant on – 'addicted' to – ECB funding, while the governments become reliant on bank funding. In the event, both governments and banks will find it very difficult to return to the market and become dependent on ECB funds.

Generous credit from the ECB to large numbers of banks in single countries, which are confronted with net payment outflows as a result of continuing current account deficits and additional capital account deficits due to a loss of domestic and foreign private sector funding, also entails a transfer of credit risk from the private sector to the official sector in countries receiving these payments. As discussed in Chapter 6, outgoing payments from banks in one country to those in another are routed through the euro area's interbank payment system TARGET2, where national central banks are the agents for their banks and the ECB acts as a clearing house. When there are more outgoing than incoming payments in a country, the imbalance leads to a debit position of the national central bank in TARGET2; conversely, when there are more incoming than outgoing payments, the national central bank gets a credit position. With the remaining AAA-rated countries in the euro area (Germany, Netherlands, Finland and Luxembourg) receiving more incoming than outgoing payments as a result of current account surpluses, the credit position of these countries in TARGET2 exceeded EUR 1 trillion in the middle of 2012. These claims are only secured with collateral of often dubious quality, delivered by banks in the other countries to obtain ECB credit. All in all, trying to avoid playing the role of lender of last resort by hoping to funnel liquidity into governments through banks creates more cost than benefit. Otmar Issing is absolutely right that 'stressing the role of the central bank as the ultimate buyer of public debt should be seen as an indication of the pathological state of public finances, not as a sign of strength'. But from this it does not follow that therefore the central bank should refuse to be the ultimate buyer of government bonds. On the contrary, as public finances are in a pathological state, the central bank needs to be available as a buyer of last resort, observing all the safeguards I have discussed extensively in this chapter.

Chapter 9

The Politics of Euro Rescue

'If the euro fails, Europe fails.'

—Angela Merkel, chancellor of the Federal
Republic of Germany, in 2011[1]

Unfortunately, the absence of defined crisis management procedures, an insufficient understanding of the deep-seated nature of the euro crisis and a lack of leadership have made effective management of the crisis and repairs of EMU's faulty architecture rather difficult. Clearly, without a determined leader, it is very difficult to take important decisions in European monetary affairs in a union of 17 states. Hence, as the euro crisis evolved, politicians, financial market participants and the general public have looked with increasing impatience to Germany, the largest (and recently strongest) country in EMU, for leadership. In addition, many policymakers at the European and national level have expected substantial financial contributions from Germany on the grounds that EMU has created economic benefits for Germany in the past. Unsurprisingly, German politicians and the electorate have seen this differently. Moreover, for historical reasons, Germany has been rather reluctant to assume the role of political leadership in

Europe. Against this background, the strategy of German policymakers has been to tie any financial support to strict conditions and share the leadership with France. However, the French and German leaders have been pulled in different directions by their electorates. While the French electorate has been more sympathetic to the demands for help by countries in financial difficulties, the German electorate has been keen on limiting financial transfers to other EMU member countries. As a result, the leaders of both countries have often been forced to make ineffective compromises on important issues. In a first phase that lasted roughly from early 2010, when Greece started to apply for financial help from its partners, to mid-2011, Chancellor Merkel appeared to put the emphasis in crisis management on containing the costs to Germany. Following a widely publicized call for a more pro-European policy by Merkel's mentor, former chancellor Helmut Kohl, she paid more attention to fortifying the institutional architecture of EMU. In the course of this second phase of German European policy, her cooperation with French president Sarkozy, which in the past had not been without friction, became much closer. However, in view of France's inherent economic weakness and the president's political impotence, it became increasingly clear that France was playing second fiddle. Germany's emergence as the hegemon in EMU has developed into a risk for the political cohesion of Europe. Let's now have a look at these points in more detail.

Outside Germany it is commonly held that Germany has been the main beneficiary of the euro. A collapse of the euro would hurt Germany most among all member countries. Had Germany not been a member of the euro, its exchange rate would have been much stronger, and hence its growth lower and unemployment rate higher, than it has been since the beginning of EMU. If Germany left the euro now, its exchange rate would surge and plunge the country into recession. Continued upward pressure on the exchange rate of the new German currency would keep the German economy on its knees for the indefinite future. Hence, in view of these large benefits from EMU membership, it would seem only fair that Germany should bear the brunt of the financial burden to save EMU. The resistance of the German electorate to having more German tax money transferred to other EMU states and the tough position of Chancellor Merkel in the negotiation of bailout programmes for suffering countries would be short-sighted and selfish.

A study by McKinsey & Company, issued at the beginning of 2012, attempted to substantiate this view.[2] McKinsey estimated that EMU, between its inception and 2010, generated benefits of EUR 330 billion, equivalent to 3.6 per cent of GDP, for its members (Table 9.1). The main beneficiary was Germany, with a gain of EUR 165 billion or 6.6 per cent of GDP. For Italy, gains were estimated at 3.1 per cent of GDP, and for France only 0.7 per cent. The study identified four sources of benefits from the euro. The first (dubbed 'technical') was cost saving from a reduction of transaction and hedging costs that can be compared to a tax on trade.[3] The second ('trade') arose from the GDP effects of an intensification of intra-EMU trade – a rough estimate of the effects of gains from trade through specialization. The third source of benefits ('competitiveness') reflected increased economic efficiency that, in the words of the authors of the study, 'were not offset by an appreciation of their currency against their trade partners, as would have been the case under flexible exchange rates'.[4] The fourth and last source of benefits ('interest rates') arose from a generally lower, and for certain countries much lower, level

Table 9.1. Approximate gains from EMU (2010, in % of GDP)

Sources	EMU-17	France	Germany	Italy
Technical	0.4	0.4	0.4	0.4
Trade	1.1	0.4	1.2	0.3
Competitiveness	0.0	−1.1	4.6	−2.0
Interest rates	2.1	1.0	0.4	4.4
Total	3.6	0.7	6.6	3.1

Source: McKinsey, 'The future of the euro', January 2012

of capital market rates. For EMU as a whole, the biggest gains, according to the study, came from lower interest rates and the GDP effects of more intra-EMU trade.

However, when Germany is declared the winner in the competition for gains from the euro, it will be a pyrrhic victory. To explain, let's first consider the commonly held view exposed above and the results of the McKinsey study. An implicit assumption about Germany's benefits from the euro is that a weak currency is a good thing. From the point of view of economics, however, this is a fallacy. A weak currency implies weak terms of trade and hence a modest level of economic welfare. In other words, when the exchange rate of a country is weak the residents have to produce and exchange more of their products against imports than in a situation where the exchange rate is strong. A weak exchange rate is therefore not a good thing for consumers who want to buy imports from abroad.

Why is it then that so many governments want the exchange rate of their country to be weak? The answer is that a weak exchange rate benefits existing companies that want to sell their products abroad. In the short term this is good for exports and therefore for domestic production and employment. Most governments care mainly for the short term and hence tend to prefer weak exchange rates to strong ones. In the long term, however, a weak exchange rate discriminates against new companies wanting to come up with new products, better technologies or more efficient production methods. A weak exchange rate keeps incumbent companies in business, even if they produce outdated products in inefficient ways, as they can sell these products abroad at a discount and still make money in domestic currency terms. It protects the owners and employees of these companies at the cost of consumer welfare and new, innovative entrepreneurs who have to compete with the existing companies for capital, labour and raw materials. In contrast, a strong exchange rate forces companies to constantly upgrade products, technologies and production methods or exit their business, freeing resources for new companies adding more value. As a result, countries with strong exchange rates tend to have more innovative industries using more up-to-date technologies to produce products that consumers like and therefore can be sold at a premium price.

To say that Germany benefited from the euro because EMU membership kept Germany's exchange rate lower than it would otherwise have been is therefore inaccurate. The weaker currency only created windfall gains for existing companies, their employees and their owners and removed pressure on these companies to upgrade their products and production technologies. Fortunately, German companies did not rely on euro weakness and hence have continued to innovate and upgrade their technologies. Since the break-up of the Bretton Woods system of exchange rates in the early 1970s, the German currency has appreciated on trend, forcing German companies to innovate and raise efficiency. Sudden bursts of exchange rate appreciation have of course been painful and regularly triggered calls for the central bank to step in and smooth exchange rate developments. However, the Bundesbank rarely heeded these calls and in the event its strong currency policy was beneficial for both capital and labour in Germany. Therefore, a weak currency cannot be in the interest of Germany, and if the euro would turn into a distinctly soft currency, exit from EMU might in the long run be economically more beneficial for Germany than remaining in EMU, despite the undoubtedly high immediate costs created by such an event. The overall positive experience with the D-Mark, which appreciated on trend against a number of currencies including the US dollar, has established a preference for a strong currency in the mind of the German electorate, giving the government a mandate to take Germany out of EMU if the euro would turn into a soft currency.

Let's now have a closer look at the results of the McKinsey study of the gains from EMU for Germany. It is interesting to note that 88 per cent of the gains from EMU estimated for Germany arrive through an expansion of trade and an increase in competitiveness. The remaining gains are attributed in equal parts to savings in hedging and transaction costs and interest rates. While the former is a direct result of the elimination of exchange rate risk, the latter is highly speculative. Would interest rates in Germany really have been higher if the country had kept the D-Mark? The case of Switzerland, where interest rates have remained consistently below German rates, suggests that this may not have been the case. The attribution of Germany's gains in competitiveness to the euro, the largest benefits from EMU identified by the McKinsey study, assumes that the Schröder government would not have implemented its Agenda 2010 programme of economic reforms if the euro had not existed. But this is not convincing. On the contrary, if the D-Mark had continued to exist and appreciated against other European currencies, like the Swiss franc did, the pressure for economic reform would certainly have been no less. The authors of the McKinsey study say that the fruits of these reforms were not eaten up by exchange rate appreciation thanks to the existence of the euro. However, as I explained above, this assertion is based on an untenable view of the economic benefits of a weak exchange rate. Had the exchange rate appreciated, the gains from enhanced competitiveness would have been more equally distributed among consumers and companies and not only benefited the latter. Finally, the gains from increased intra-EMU trade identified in the McKinsey study are unfortunately associated with the build-up of very large current account imbalances, which have led to a balance-of-payments crisis in EMU. Hence, it seems rather dubious to count the expansion of imbalanced trade flows as a benefit from EMU. Could EMU perhaps have helped German exporters to better exploit economies of scale and hence to raise productivity? The fact that German companies expanded trade with emerging market economies much more than with their EMU partners over the last decade would argue against this proposition. The bottom line is that only the savings of hedging and transaction costs in the amount of 0.4 per cent of GDP can be safely classified as hard and lasting gains for Germany from EMU. I arrive at a similar, rather sceptical assessment of the gains from the euro estimated by the McKinsey study for the euro area as a whole. The gains attributed to interest rate reduction and trade expansion were associated with the build-up of serious imbalances in EMU member countries (e.g., house price bubbles and unsustainable current account imbalances), which now threaten the existence of EMU. As in Germany's case, the hard and lasting gain seems to

Chart 9.1. GDP per capita of EMU member countries

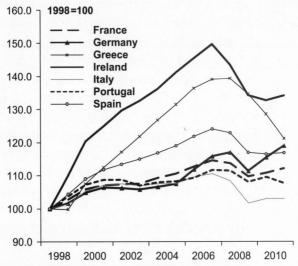

Source: Haver Analytics, Deutsche Bank Research

result from the reduction in hedging and transaction costs in intra-EMU trade. At 0.4 per cent of GDP, these gains seem moderate and may not cover the costs of redressing the macroeconomic imbalances built up during the first decade of EMU.

A simple way to gauge the gains from EMU for individual member countries is to look at the relative performance of their per capita GDP since the introduction of EMU. As Chart 9.1 shows, until the beginning of the financial crisis in 2007 that turned into the euro crisis as of 2010, Germany's GDP per capita performed at the lower end of the range of countries considered here (the GIIPS group, France and Germany). Initially, the clear beneficiaries were Ireland, Greece and Spain, which benefited from sharply lower interest rates (see Chart 9.2) and experienced a credit-fuelled boom of private and public consumption and housing investment. Only more recently, as the

Chart 9.2. Long-term interest rates of selected EMU member countries

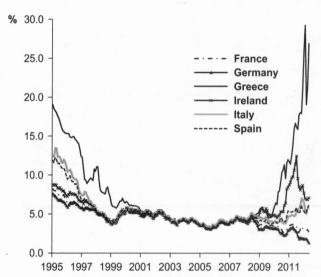

Source: Haver Analytics, Deutsche Bank Research

financial and euro crisis has pushed countries with large internal and external financial deficits into recession, have some of the gains of the peripheral countries been unwound. Still, even Greece has not yet entirely lost the gains in GDP per capita achieved relative to Germany since the introduction of the euro. In Ireland, which is receiving credit support from the European Community and the IMF, the level of GDP per capital in 2011 was still above that of Germany.

Would Germany have performed even worse had it not been a member of EMU? I also have doubts that this would have been the case. European countries outside EMU, such as the UK or Sweden, have on balance performed better than Germany. But would a German currency outside EMU really have behaved in a way comparable to the UK pound or the Swedish kroner? Many people may

Chart 9.3. GDP per capita in Germany and Switzerland

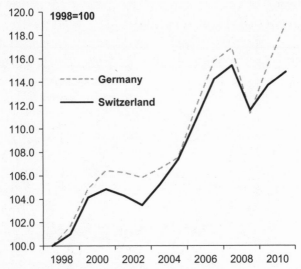

Source: Haver Analytics, Deutsche Bank Research

doubt this. Perhaps it would have behaved more like the Swiss franc, which in past foreign exchanges often traded in a similar way as the D-Mark. Did the Swiss economy suffer from the fact that the franc was not a member of EMU? The performance of Swiss per capita GDP suggests that this was not the case. As Chart 9.3 shows, Swiss GDP per capita did not develop very differently from its German equivalent.

All in all, it is difficult to identify the hard and lasting economic benefits from EMU beyond the moderate gains from savings on transaction costs in intra-EMU trade, which were already estimated in the early 1990s. The actual benefits from EMU are indeed more political than economic. The motivation for the creation of EMU was of a political nature. EMU was seen as another – perhaps the last – stepping stone to the political union of Europe, as explained in Chapter 1. It was a vision developed by post–World War II politicians to safeguard peace in Europe and, more recently, to secure Europe's political place in a world more and more dominated by the US and China. As a project bringing political benefits for Europe, the euro can still be defended. As a means for raising economic welfare, EMU is much less convincing. For Germany as well, the benefits must be sought in the political domain. To claim that Germany reaps large economic gains from the euro may be politically correct but is not convincing from an economic point of view. Against this background, it seems important that economic efforts to stabilize EMU do not undermine the perception that a common currency is politically desirable in strong countries giving financial support as well as in weak countries receiving it.

Chancellor Merkel's initial reaction to the euro crisis was guided by the desire to keep the cost to German taxpayers low. Assistance to illiquid EMU partner countries was to be extended only under strict conditions regarding their future course of economic policy and, if the country proved to be insolvent, with the financial participation of private-sector creditors. Thus, as she feared that the European Commission would be too soft on the country, Merkel insisted on the involvement of the IMF in the rescue operation for Greece that started in April 2010. When it became clear that Greece's debt burden was unsustainable, she insisted in mid-2011 on partial debt forgiveness by private creditors. Although the insistence on comprehensive adjustment efforts by the Greek government and the eventual debt restructuring was fully justified, particularly in view of the size of the country's internal and external economic imbalances, the slow and sometimes erratic development of the policy towards Greece created a high degree of uncertainty in financial markets and contributed to the contagion to other markets for sovereign bonds.

In August 2011, former Chancellor Helmut Kohl gave a rare interview in which he indirectly complained that the policy course of the Merkel government lacked a clear orientation. With regard to European policy, Kohl admonished his successor and mentee: 'What Europe needs in this crisis is a proactive approach and a bundle of forward-looking, wisely balanced and pragmatic measures designed to bring Europe and the euro back on a healthy path and to secure them for the future.'[5] Although Chancellor Merkel initially did not react to Kohl's intervention, it seems that it had an impact on her approach to crisis management. In the autumn of 2011, she initiated a revision of the EU treaty, incorporating rules committing EMU member countries to strict fiscal discipline. At the same time, she declared that private sector participation in the restructuring of Greek's public debt was 'exceptional and unique' and would not be repeated in other countries. She also backed the Bundesbank in its resistance against any access of the existing or future crisis management mechanisms, the EFSF and the ESM, to credits from the central bank. Merkel's new approach to crisis management extended her initial course with an emphasis on fortifying EMU's institutional architecture and the attempt to rebuild trust in EMU among the German electorate and financial market participants. Trust of the electorate was to be recouped by incorporating earlier pledges to fiscal discipline (in the context of the Stability and Growth Pact, which turned out to be unenforceable) into legally binding treaties, with the possibility to sue violators in the European Court of Justice.

The government's backing of the Bundesbank's unconditional rejection of any lending by the central bank to governments, even as a measure of last resort to avert financial collapse, was probably influenced by the

Chart 9.4. Germany: The decline of D-Mark nostalgia

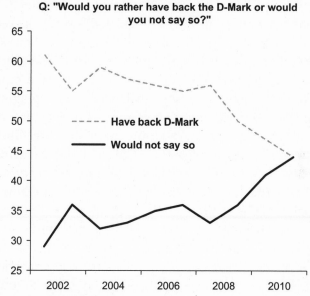

Q: "Would you rather have back the D-Mark or would you not say so?"

- - - - - Have back D-Mark

———— Would not say so

Source: IfD Allensbach, 2011

national trauma created by hyperinflation in 1923, which made such operations highly suspicious in the eyes of the electorate. In view of their historical experience with the debasement of money in the early 1920s and currency reform in 1948, the Germans are very sensitive with regard to the stability of money. Hence, anything that could be seen as endangering the value of money raises suspicion. Thus, the ECB's decision to buy government bonds in the secondary market undermined trust in the new central bank, which had slowly built up during the first decade of EMU. As Chart 9.4 shows, in 2002, more than 60 per cent of Germans polled by the Allensbach Institute still wanted to have the D-Mark back. By 2011, the share of those longing for the good old D-Mark had declined to 44 per cent and matched the share of those who were content with the euro.

Therefore, an institutional arrangement allowing access of governments to central bank funds, even if restricted to emergency situations and extended by a crisis management institution against policy conditionality, was considered politically inopportune by the German government. German private sector economists tended to concur with this position, declaring any credit from the central bank to the government as inconsistent with the principles of 'Ordnungspolitik': a school of thought little known outside Germany that puts great emphasis on a sound institutional structure with a view to setting incentives for economic efficiency and price stability. Unfortunately, however, the defenders of the principles of 'Ordnungspolitik' failed to answer the question of who could lend to a distressed government in a liquidity crisis, if not the central bank. Finally, trust of financial market participants was to be restored in Merkel's new approach by promising that debt restructuring for Greece would not be repeated for other countries. Unsurprisingly, in view of the changes in the official position on debt restructuring in Greece, financial markets did not find this promise entirely credible. By playing down debt restructuring in the future and pushing for tighter fiscal rules, Merkel opted for political means instead of market pressure for the enforcement of fiscal discipline. Her decision may have been influenced by the view that markets failed to exert a disciplinary influence on fiscal policy during the first decade of EMU. Yet market pressure has been essential since 2009 for pushing governments towards fiscal adjustment and structural reform. Hence, any new architecture for EMU that does not give markets a pivotal role in enforcing economic and fiscal policy discipline would seem incomplete and thus not credible.

Table 9.2. Financial indicators in main EMU countries

	(% of GDP, 2011)			
	Public debt	Private debt	Public deficit	Current account
France	98.6	129.0	5.2	−2.1
Italy	118.4	162.6	3.8	−3.1
Germany	86.9	124.8	4.3	5.6

Source: Haver Analytics, OECD, Deutsche Bank Research

In France (and some other mostly southern European countries) there has been a much greater willingness by the electorate to support financially troubled countries. However, this is probably not reflective of a more generous disposition in French taxpayers, but has been influenced by the feeling that their country is fundamentally not so different from those in need of assistance. Indeed, when compared with Italy and Germany, France seemed to stand somewhere in the middle as far the state of government finances and the external current account balance are concerned (see Table 9.2). The feeling that 'in the end the Germans will pay' – a line that could often be heard at the time during coffee breaks in conferences on the euro crisis – may also have played a role in taking a more liberal view on official credit to countries in trouble. From the more rational point of view of economics, the support by France and other southern European states for more troubled countries and the associated initial rejection of German wishes for a restructuring of the private debt of Greece, could also be explained by their desire to retain the status as an issuer of 'risk-free' assets for every government in the euro area. Following the default of an EMU country – even if it was an obviously insolvent country – markets were likely to trade only German debt as 'risk-free' and to regard all other sovereign debt as 'credit', a fear that indeed materialized after debt restructuring for Greece was announced.

With respect to the involvement of the ECB in extending credit to troubled governments through purchases of government bonds in the secondary market, attitudes in France and elsewhere have also been more relaxed than in Germany. In these countries, there is a strong tradition of regarding the central bank as subservient to the government, hence the inclination to have the central bank step in when the capital markets are closed to the government.

Endowed with different political mandates from home, the French president and German chancellor often had to strike compromises at the European level that disappointed both observers and market participants and reinforced the impression of ineffective crisis management. For instance, a compromise was reached in July 2011 for persuading private creditors to take a 'voluntary' haircut of 21 per cent on their holdings of Greek government bonds. The compromise appeared to be a 'fudge', as the haircut was neither voluntary nor sufficient to restore the Greek government to solvency. In December of the same year, the terms were changed to a cut of the nominal claims by 50 per cent, which was later turned into a reduction of the net present value of outstanding Greek government bonds by more than 70 per cent, due to the structuring of the exchange of outstanding Greek debt against new debt issued by the EFSF and Greece. Again, the deal was supposed to be 'voluntary' and the haircut did not seem enough to restore solvency for the Greek government. In the event, the nominal haircut was even bigger (53.5 per cent) and the loss of the net present value of claims on Greece more severe (around 75 per cent). Moreover, investors found themselves subordinated to the ECB, which escaped its haircut through an exchange of the bonds they had acquired under their Securities Markets Programme (aimed at 'restoring the transmission mechanism of monetary policy') against new Greek bonds.[6] With private investors having been subordinated to both the IMF and the ECB and forced to swallow ever-larger haircuts in the case of Greece, the outlook diminished for other countries having received IMF and ECB help to return to the market.

Governments were also obsessed with fears of contagion by other sovereign debt and a deepening of the financial crisis, in case they triggered a default rating of Greek government debt by the rating agencies or a 'credit event' in the credit default swap market that led to the payout of credit insurance. The desire to avoid the payment of credit insurance was another factor preventing clear decisions and creating the impression that leaders were driven by the financial markets. It also had unwelcome consequences. The attempt to prevent a payout by pushing for 'voluntary' debt restructuring raised questions about the value of sovereign debt insurance and induced investors to sell euro area government bonds, which they had previously regarded as insured against default. It may also have soured investors' attitudes towards bond insurance offered by the EFSF, which was intended to make these bonds more attractive. How credible was such official insurance when governments were busy trying to prevent private bond insurance from paying out? In the event, all the concerns about the effects of triggering payments on credit insurance proved unfounded. When the Greek government retroactively introduced collective action clauses in its bonds issued under Greek law, so as to raise the participation rate of private investors in the debt restructuring, the International Swaps and Derivatives Association (ISDA) diagnosed a 'credit event' that would be covered under credit insurance. On 19 March 2012, a net payment of EUR 2.5 billion (EUR 3.2 billion credit insurance minus EUR 0.7 billion recovery value) was made to investors who had bought credit default swaps on Greek sovereign debt. There were no glitches and markets were unperturbed by the event.

Greece was also responsible for breaking the taboo of contemplating exit from EMU. Against the background of a further deterioration of economic conditions in Greece through the first few months of 2012, elections were held in May. After two rounds, a government finally emerged with a mandate from the electorate to renegotiate the adjustment programme just agreed with the IMF and euro area institutions. The aim of the new Greek government was to obtain additional funds so as to be able to extend the period for fiscal adjustment. This created a serious dilemma for both the IMF and the euro area institutions. On the one hand, the demand of the Greeks did not seem unreasonable given the disastrous economic situation. On the other hand, those providing adjustment funding could no longer ignore that the adjustment programme was not working and that they were risking throwing good money after bad. As a result, a public debate about a Greek exit from EMU, dubbed 'Grexit', ensued. At the time, I suggested that there was a way between staying in the EMU and leaving it.[7] Since the Greek population had no intention to exit EMU and no country could be thrown out, a formal exit of Greece was very unlikely. At the same time, neither the IMF nor euro area institutions could afford to provide continuous adjustment funding when adjustment seemed almost impossible. The solution to this dilemma in my view was for the euro area to stop funding Greek primary government budget deficits but to keep providing funds for debt service payments (to avoid a complete default of the Greek government, now also on its public creditors) and for the restructuring of the banking sector in a European restructuring regime (so as to avoid a complete collapse of banking services and hence an economic, political and social meltdown). Should the Greek government continue to run primary budget deficits, they would have to issue IOUs to their creditors, including pensioners and civil servants, which would assume the role of a parallel currency. When wages were paid in this parallel currency, which I dubbed the 'Geuro', there was even a chance to regain cost competitiveness, as the Geuro would almost certainly trade at a steep discount against the euro. Considering the press echo triggered by my note in both Germany and Greece, public opinion had shifted towards expecting Greece to loosen its ties with EMU in one way or another.

Over time, weak compromises at the European level eroded leaders' credibility at home and in the financial markets. Similarly, efforts at returning effectively insolvent countries to the capital markets on the basis of tough economic adjustment programmes failed and destroyed confidence in the ability of politicians to manage the crisis. Thus, what initially looked like a problem at the fringes of EMU that could probably have been resolved with determined action (e.g., by a swift restructuring of the excessively high public debt in Greece) mushroomed into an existential crisis of EMU. The loss of confidence caused a run on all but the strongest bond markets of EMU governments and created the risk of a run on banks and deposit flight from EMU countries with balance-of-payment deficits. Clearly, should the latter ever occur the odds of a break-up of EMU would rise to truly worrisome levels.

Germany's recovered economic strength and the need for a leader through the euro crisis has pushed the German government towards an increasingly assertive political role in the management of the crisis. At the same time, France's inherent economic weakness has reduced it to second fiddle in the leadership couple. With the German electorate having little sympathy for the view that they are obliged to help others, due to alleged benefits they haven't felt, and therefore providing assistance only against conditions that appear harsh in the eyes of its recipients, the German government has more and more appeared to play the role of the hegemon in the monetary union. This has created a rift in the club of euro area countries and even Europe as a whole. In Germany, resentment has grown against ever-increasing financial demands from partner countries; in recipient countries, resentment has increased against Germany as the power dictating economic austerity; and in France uncertainty has risen about the country's role in Europe. Crisis management has even endangered key democratic principles. The affairs of the debtor countries have to a considerable degree been managed by international technocrats or been influenced by political pressure from creditor countries. In the latter, parliaments have been pushed to hand over money for support programmes by 'experts' claiming that disaster would strike if they did not comply. 'At the end, some parliament always approves', complains Martin Schulz, president of the European Parliament. 'In the meantime, however, governments act and confront the members of parliaments with hard facts. We can only sign off on the decisions by the European Council. We see how resistance against this grows in the Bundestag.'[8] At the same time, efforts to rebuild the institutional architecture of EMU have separated EMU countries from non-EMU countries. At the European Council meeting of 9 December 2011, the UK vetoed a revision of the EU treaties to include stricter and more binding clauses enforcing fiscal discipline and thus forced the remaining countries to conclude a separate treaty (dubbed Treaty on Stability, Coordination and Governance (TSCG)). Thus, the political management of the euro crisis has added to the erosion of the political cohesion of EU and EMU members that began with the fall of the Berlin Wall. Yet a reversal of this process and a strengthening of political cohesion are essential to prevent a failure and break-up of EMU.

As Italy and Spain slipped into recession in 2012, a debate on the merits of rigorous structural reform and fiscal adjustment started. German policymakers and economists came under fire from their peers abroad for allegedly killing economic growth by demanding too much reform and adjustment from deficit countries in too short a period of time. At the political level, the campaign against euro area economic policies inspired by Germany was led by France's new president, François Hollande, who called for a revision of the fiscal compact with a view to easing pressure for strict fiscal discipline, the introduction of eurobonds to fund investment projects ('project bonds') and the pursuit of a more expansionary monetary policy by the ECB to stimulate growth and help governments struggling to service their debt and fund deficits. In a development very similar to the birth of the Stability and Growth Pact in the 1990s, this led to the addition of a French-inspired growth pact to the fiscal pact championed by Chancellor Merkel at the European Council meeting of June 27–8.

Those stressing the need for reform and adjustment, which unsurprisingly includes this author, retort that the critics of these policies, especially those at the political level, seem to subscribe to a rather mechanistic concept of economic growth. From national accounting identities, it follows of course that higher consumption, investment and net exports raise GDP. If private demand is weak, the identity suggests that public or export demand ought to be raised to support GDP. Assuming that there is limited scope to influence exports in the short term, the natural conclusion seems to be that it is up to public consumption and investment to support growth. Hence, policies of public deficit reduction appear to undermine growth.

But this view, like most traditional economic models used to calculate 'fiscal multipliers', neglects the crucial role of confidence – some would say 'animal spirits' – for economic growth. Confidence is needed for companies to invest, banks to lend and consumers to spend. Without the confidence of households, bankers and entrepreneurs, any increase in public consumption and investment has, in the best-case scenario, a temporary effect on growth; in the worst case, the resulting deterioration of public finances can destroy confidence of private economic agents and have a lasting negative impact on growth. Hence, the most important task for an economic policy aimed at fighting recession would seem to be to restore confidence of domestic residents and foreign investors in economic and financial soundness, even if this implies temporary output losses caused by fiscal austerity and structural reform. Fiscal austerity is needed to restore confidence in the sustainability of government finances, stabilization and restructuring of the banking sector is needed to rebuild confidence in the financial sector, and structural reform is needed to improve external competitiveness and restore confidence in the external solvency. Confidence not only supports investment by companies and avoids an increase of savings by households out of fear for the future, but it also induces lending by domestic and foreign private financial institutions. As a result, there is less pressure for the immediate reduction of internal and external deficits and a lesser need for public adjustment funding by EU institutions and the IMF. The question therefore is not whether to give priority to fiscal austerity or economic growth, as it has been phrased by some politicians and economists, but to find the optimal degree of austerity and structural reforms for the maximization of confidence.

As so often in the history of the EU, the politics of euro rescue in the event turned into a fundamental discussion between Germany and France on the final destination of the European project. The German government pursued the line that joint liability for government debt beyond limited amounts for helping to fund adjustment could only follow much deeper political integration. For Chancellor Merkel, a shift of financial liability to the European level was not acceptable without a commensurate shift of sovereignty and strictly binding commitments to debt reduction. For French president Hollande, as for his predecessors, relinquishing key elements of sovereignty in the financial affairs of the nation was out of the question. At the same time, he supported the desire of southern European countries to keep market access open and ease their interest burden through issuance of debt under joint and several liability. In view of the hitherto relatively low risk premium on French government bonds, the position of the president appeared to reflect his fear that France was unable to revert the trend of rising public indebtedness and would sooner or later have to rely on the creditworthiness of Germany to retain market access at reasonable interest rates. The political stalemate between France and Germany on this issue has left only one way to mutualize the debt of

sovereigns or banks in EMU in times of extreme financial
stress: the absorption of this debt on the balance sheet of
the ECB. With Germany and her allies commanding only
a minority of votes in the ECB's Governing Council, the
country could only escape debt mutualization through the
backdoor of the ECB's balance sheet when it left the euro.
But would this not be completely impossible? I'll return to
this question in Chapter 11.

Chapter 10

Why Europe Needs the Euro

'Europe does not need the euro.'

—Thilo Sarrazin, former member of the board of
the Bundesbank and book author, in May 2012.[1]

In previous chapters I have argued that the conventional rationale for the euro – a catalyst for full political European union to ensure ever-lasting peace in Europe or a means to generate tangible economic benefits – stands on shaky ground. This would seem to suggest that the strongest arguments for keeping the euro are the political and economic costs created by its dissolution. While avoiding the costs of dissolution is undoubtedly an important reason, it is in my view not the only one. If managed as nonpolitical money in an EMU where member states are liable for their sovereign financial decisions, the euro offers the participating countries the opportunity of creating a hard currency that can stand on its own against the currencies of other global economic powers. As shown by the example of Switzerland, which eventually decided to cap the exchange rate of the Swiss franc versus the euro, it can be very difficult for small countries to shield themselves from the external effects of monetary policies pursued by larger countries.[2] This has also been the experience of a number of emerging market countries, which have complained about the external effects of an easy US monetary policy on their nominal exchange and inflation rates. The Brazilian government even accused the US of waging a 'currency war' against them and other emerging market economies. A Europe of small countries with national currencies could in the future feel similarly dominated by larger foreign economic powers as the emerging market countries do today. This would be especially problematic if the present US-centric global monetary system experienced a crisis of its own. The likelihood of such a crisis during the rest of this decade is in my view fairly high. By pooling national monetary sovereignty, European countries can retain joint policy sovereignty to safeguard stability in a possibly volatile future global monetary environment.

When Richard Nixon, on 15 August 1971, declared a temporary suspension of the linkage of the US dollar to gold, he laid the ground for the emergence of the 'fiat money system' as we know it today. In this system, money is no longer tied to a material anchor but can be issued at will by the central bank. Trust in this artificially created money now solely depends on the belief that the central bank will maintain its purchasing power for goods, services and – some would add – real assets. Although Nixon justified his move with the aim to end a sequence of financial crises, on which he blamed the gold link of the dollar, the system he launched experienced numerous crises of its own and may eventually turn out to be inherently unstable.

The first phase of the young fiat money system – I call it the period of 'de-anchored money' – was very volatile. Most central banks – with the notable exception of the

Bundesbank and the Swiss National Bank – accommodated the oil price shock in the wake of the 1974 war in the Middle East. They could not prevent a severe recession with this, but as the economy recovered the initial jump in the general price level induced by the rise in oil prices turned into a price-wage-price spiral. Inflation rose in the following years while economic growth remained volatile and below the levels of the 1960s. The term 'stagflation' was coined to capture the worrisome combination of dissatisfactory growth and rising inflation. The deeper reasons for stagflation were the economic rigidities that hindered a rapid economic adjustment to the relative price changes induced by the oil price increase and the central bankers' lack of understanding of the role of stable inflation expectations in the anchoring of the fiat money system. Global economic conditions deteriorated markedly further as governments and central banks continued their constructivist policies aimed at stimulating economic growth and oil prices surged again towards the end of the 1970s. There was much talk of the global monetary system going through a major crisis at the annual IMF meeting in Belgrade in October 1979.

Paul Volcker, who attended the meeting in his capacity as the newly appointed chairman of the Federal Reserve, cut his stay in Belgrade short and returned to Washington with the firm determination to break the vicious inflation spiral. To re-anchor the fiat money system, he borrowed a leaf from the book of the monetarists, who had gained in public recognition during the stagflationary 1970s. Pursuit of a numerical target for the growth of the money stock provided the opportunity for Volcker to tie down monetary expansion through a restrictive monetary policy and so to quell inflation. The break of inflation dynamics came at the cost of a severe recession in 1981–2. But after the experience of the 1970s, the American public was so fed up with inflation that it supported Volcker's harsh policies despite loud opposition by several powerful lobby groups.[3] Unfortunately, however, the new anchor for the fiat money system did not hold for long. Owing to financial innovation, such as money market funds and other money-like financial instruments, it quickly became very difficult to define 'money' in banks' balance sheets. Hence, already under Volcker, the Federal Reserve moved away from money targeting. It abandoned it entirely under Alan Greenspan, and it even ceased to publish the broad money aggregate M3 under Ben Bernanke.

In mid-1987, Greenspan took over from Volcker as chairman. His first test came quickly with the stock market crash of September 1987 and he passed it with flying colours. The crash awakened memories of 1929, but Greenspan countered any downside risks for the real economy with an aggressive easing of monetary policy. We shall never know whether this move was necessary to prevent an economic downturn or whether the economy would simply have shrugged off the decline in stock prices. But, as public discussion tends to seek causality, the Federal Reserve received the credit for having saved the economy. This laid the ground for a general policy rule followed in later years: the central bank refrains from leaning against asset price increases but stands ready to save the financial sector and the economy when asset price bubbles burst. Financial market participants tellingly called this the 'Greenspan Put'. Between 1987 and 2006 we saw an extraordinary expansion of credit and the emergence of what I call the credit economy. This was mainly possible for two reasons. First, risk taking in financial markets was encouraged by the feeling that central banks could control financial downside risks and the low policy rates sustained by the major central banks of the world over a prolonged period of time. As implicit or explicit inflation targeting became the policy approach of most central banks and as inflation was depressed by higher productivity resulting from technical progress and global trade integration, the cost of funds was generally kept below the return to capital, which induced asset price and real investment booms (often in the real estate sector). Second, financial innovation in the credit markets depersonalized credit relations. The old risk management rule of 'know-your-customer' in traditional banking was replaced by securitization of credit and the clever engineering of financial products, where risky single assets were aggregated into an asset pool with seemingly low risk. This alchemy of finance created generous real gains for the alchemists and paper gains for the investors. It also allowed for credit extension around the world and the creation of a truly global credit economy.

The intellectual background to the macroeconomic policy regime of the last few decades was the fusion of New Keynesian with neoclassical economic theories. This economic paradigm (let's call it the NKNC model) combined the constructivist approach to economic policies favoured by the New Keynesians with the love of the neoclassical economists for general equilibrium theories and efficient markets. Since the model assigned the financial sector only a passive role, activist economic policies were combined with a laissez-faire approach to the financial industry. This allowed the latter to develop highly sophisticated financial products based on modern portfolio and efficient market theory. At the same time, directly or indirectly central banks pursued numerical targets for inflation and set their policy rates for this purpose according to the Taylor Rule. According to this rule, the central bank rate is given by a long-term, cyclically neutral real rate and the expected

Chart 10.1. US output gap and credit growth

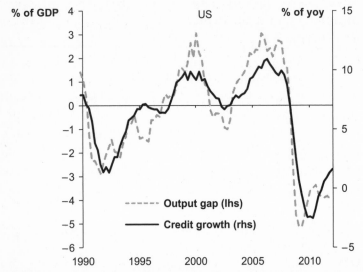

Source: M. Biggs and T. Mayer, 'Towards a macro-prudential policy framework', Global Economic Perspectives, Deutsche Bank, 6 June 2012

(or target) inflation rate, adjusted for deviations of actual real GDP from its potential (the output gap) and deviations of inflation from target. Unfortunately, the combination of constructivist monetary policies with a laissez-faire approach to the financial sector turned out to be inherently unstable. This is illustrated in Chart 10.1, which shows the output gap and credit growth for the US – I introduced a similar chart for the euro area in Chapter 4. The reader will find two points interesting here: first, there has been a strong and stable correlation between the output gap and credit growth; second, an output gap of zero has gone along with nominal credit growth of 7 per cent. From this follows that a monetary policy that succeeded in eliminating cyclical fluctuations by ensuring a zero output gap accommodated credit growth about two percentage points above nominal

GDP growth. In other words, the period of the Great Moderation – the two decades since the early 1990s with minimal cyclical fluctuations – turned a blind eye to an ever-increasing ratio of credit to GDP, which was bound to lead to financial instability and eventual collapse.

In contrast to the New Keynesian–neoclassical fusion model, the Austrian school of economics offered a more sombre view of the period of the Great Moderation. According to Austrian business cycle theory, the manipulation of funding costs and insurance of financial risks by the central banks induced the emergence of investment and asset price bubbles in the bond, equity and, eventually, real estate markets.[4] Since real estate is the asset attracting most leverage and as real estate prices rose across a broad range of countries, the real estate bubble was associated with a credit bubble and hence the most dangerous one of all. It started to burst with the collapse of subprime credit products in the US mortgage market in early 2007. What, according to Federal Reserve chairman Bernanke, at the time looked like an accident in a small segment of the US mortgage market quickly turned into a global financial crisis. The collapse of the US investment bank Lehman Brothers in September 2008 raised the spectre of deflation and depression along the lines of the 1930s and triggered a powerful counterattack by central banks. Policy rates were cut and balance sheets massively increased as the central banks stepped between creditors (mainly the investing public) and debtors (mainly banks and governments) to stabilize credit relationships and avoid a meltdown in the form of 'debt deflation'. The balance sheets of central banks expanded to hitherto unknown sizes (Chart 10.1). As they propped up failing banks and (as of 2010 in Europe) failing governments, we entered into what I call the central bank money economy.

Chart 10.2. A massive increase in central bank balance sheets

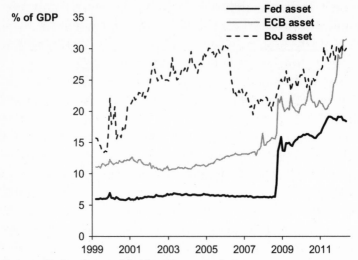

Source: National central banks, Haver Analytics

As already mentioned at the beginning of this chapter, fiat money is, of course, also only 'credit'. It is backed by the belief that central banks will issue it only to fund credit to viable banks that extend credit to viable private and public sector entities. If this is so, money is covered by the goods, services and real assets these entities produce. But if money is backing credit to economically unviable entities that fail to produce the adequate real counter-value, then the value of money itself becomes impaired. From the Olympic distance central bankers look at the micro cosmos of companies and private households operating in the 'real economy', they cannot be sure whether the expected real counter-value to money will be produced. Hence, they look at the present and prospective development of inflation for signs of whether or not this may be the case. They assure us that they will rein in money and credit as soon as there are signs that inflation is picking up. However, the assurance of central bankers to safeguard the purchasing power of money lacks credibility for two reasons. First, as is well known from the studies of the academic monetarists more than thirty years ago, money affects prices with long and variable time lags and, I would add, in a nonlinear way. In other words, money expansion has no effect for a long time, only to lead eventually to an uncontrollable rise in inflation. Since we know neither the time lag nor the quantitative relationship between central bank money growth and inflation, we are likely to experience nasty surprises at some time in the future. Second, the longer central bankers keep policy rates low and central bank balance sheets oversized, the more economic agents adjust their portfolios to this environment. Projects become unviable when monetary policy–influenced funding costs rise. The larger the number of projects threatened by a rise of funding costs, the more vulnerable the economy becomes to a tightening of monetary policy and the less able will the central bank be to counter inflationary pressures. My guess is that when inflation rises, be that as a result of an exogenous shock or an increase (often tellingly called 'unanchoring') of inflation expectations, central bankers will dither and delay in adjusting monetary policy. Hence, a graceful exit from the central bank money economy seems rather improbable. More likely is that central bankers (through interest rate policy and direct asset purchases, generally dubbed 'quantitative easing') and governments (through financial regulation) will keep nominal interest rates low and push real rates into negative territory. In the 1970s the term 'financial repression' was coined for such a policy.[5] Recently, this term has made an impressive comeback in the academic literature and public discussion.[6] In view of the present monetary policy of the Federal Reserve, which aims to keep interest rates close to zero across the entire maturity spectrum of the government bond yield curve for years to come, the US seems particularly prone to create a modern, mild form of financial repression.

What will happen when US central bankers lose control over inflation and collude with the government to create financial repression? A loss of confidence in our presently US-dominated fiat money system would seem fairly likely. In the post–World War II period there was no escape from financial repression. International capital flows were regulated and information and communication technology was an infant industry. Governments were in control and investors had no place to hide from them. Things are different today. Emerging market economies may offer safe havens when investors lose confidence in the ability of the largest global economy to reduce public and private debt to sustainable levels without debasing its currency. A new global monetary order may emerge, where emerging market currencies play a much more important role. Having lost faith in the fiat money system and abandoned the US dollar as monetary anchor by tying their own currencies to it, emerging market economies could return to a material anchor – precious metals or a basket of commodities – for the value of their moneys.

Where would Europe stand in such a new global monetary order? With each country having its own national currency, Europe would have very limited monetary sovereignty. In a world with internationally mobile capital, countries would be busy fending off downward or upward pressure on their exchange rates relative to larger emerging market currencies, the US dollar or each other's currencies. Real economies would suffer from monetary policies influenced from abroad. Against this, a Europe with a common currency would be sufficiently independent from foreign policy influences transmitted through the exchange rate.

It would have the chance to shape economic policies in its own interest and establish the euro as an equal to other important global currencies. As a counterweight to a politicized, inflationary fiat money system elsewhere, the euro would have to be reconstituted as a nonpolitical hard currency. This means that monetary policy would have to abstain from trying to manage the business cycle and propping up governments or banks in financial difficulties. Governments would have to take responsibility and be liable for their sovereign budget decisions. In other words, EMU would have to go back to its original vision. How this could be done will be the subject of the next chapter.

Chapter 11

A New Foundation
for EMU

'There are two models for Europe: Free access to the printing press, that is, Target credits, Eurobonds and political debt brakes. Europe has already implemented half of this model. The other is the American one: states can go bankrupt... This model relies on control by the market.'

—Hans-Werner Sinn, president of Ifo Economic
Research Institute, in 2012[1]

The analysis in the previous chapters suggests that a monetary union in Europe with comprehensive financial transfers between stronger and weaker states is unsustainable. It would require a strong political centre receiving the lion's share of tax revenues collected in the union and the ability to steer the political debate for the union as a whole, in other words a European government with political and financial clout similar to the federal governments of the United States or Germany. For the foreseeable future, the likelihood that a European government of this sort will emerge from the euro crisis is close to zero. More likely is a halfway house with joint liability for debt issued by EMU member states, liberal use of the money printing press to fund government debt that cannot be sold in the capital markets and futile efforts to ensure fiscal discipline of member governments by intergovernmental treaties that cannot be enforced. Sooner or later, this halfway house would collapse as economically and financially stronger countries will resist the financial exploitation through joint debt liability and inflation created by the liberal use of the money printing press.

In my view, the only way to make EMU work is to embed it into a union roughly along the lines of the United States of the mid–nineteenth century, i.e., to establish it as a federation of sovereign states where interstate fiscal transfers play only a minor role, member states are fully responsible for their financial affairs, the common currency is managed by a politically independent central bank and economic and financial crises can be effectively dealt with. There would be a transfer of political sovereignty to the supranational level, but in a limited and gradual way, in line with past practice in the context of European integration. Such a structure requires the five fundamental building blocks described in the following.

1. **Governments are fully responsible for their financial decisions**. The bulk of government revenue collection and spending occurs at the state level. The European Union receives only a small part of government revenue and therefore has only limited spending capacity. Insolvent governments must not be bailed out by the community or other governments, but be allowed to go bankrupt. If governments are not only insolvent but economies also suffer from serious overvaluation of their internal real exchange rate and therefore lack international competitiveness, and if they

are unable to create the necessary economic flexibility to engineer internal devaluations and observe a hard budget constraint, they must be allowed to exit EMU. To make default within EMU possible, government debt must eventually be reduced below the threshold at which the default of a debtor has potentially disastrous consequences for the financial system. To allow exit from EMU as a measure of last resort, EU treaties have to be changed such that a country leaving EMU can remain a member of the EU.

2. **The central bank is responsible for price stability. Since price stability cannot be achieved without financial stability, the central bank is the source for funds of last resort for all systemically important debtors.** Modern central banks tend to pursue inflation targets defined as a tolerable increase in the price for a basket of goods, bought by a typical consumer to sustain his living. Implicit in this monetary policy strategy is the assumption that economic agents always make their decisions in a rational way, and markets for goods, services and assets are always efficient. When these assumptions hold, controlling the increase of the prices for goods and services is sufficient to achieve monetary and financial stability. Prices of real and financial assets always reflect all publicly available information and hence are consistent with expected returns. All price changes are random, reflecting new information that nobody could foresee. The central bank is only called upon to act as a lender of last resort in the unlikely event of a financial 'accident', as it may arise by a random error of an economic agent. Of course, the assumptions of universally rational expectations and efficient markets do not hold, with the consequence that inflation targeting is a suboptimal strategy for monetary policy.

Central banks relying on this strategy have closed their eyes to asset price bubbles and neglected regulation aimed at limiting excesses in financial institutions, as well as in markets for financial and real assets. During the financial crisis, they had difficulties in appropriately performing the function of a lender of last resort, in some cases failing to lend in time (such as the Bank of England in the case of the bank run on Northern Rock) and in others failing to wind down emergency lending (such as the US Federal Reserve in the case of continuous purchases of government bonds during robust economic recovery). In EMU, the task of the central bank should be to safeguard the purchasing power of money by countering excessive movements in prices for goods, services and assets. Excessive price movements for assets can be countered through a policy aimed at dampening swings in the credit cycle. This requires a more restrictive stance of monetary policy in the upward phase of the credit cycle and a more expansionary stance in the downward phase. It also requires providing funds of last resort to systematically important debtors when credit markets freeze in a financial panic.

3. **To ensure that the central bank does not monetize the debt of insolvent systemically important debtors, be they banks or governments, it acts as a lender of last resort only in close cooperation with the European Systemic Risk Board (ESRB) and a EMF.** The ESRB was created toward the end of 2010 for the macroprudential surveillance of the financial sector in the European Union. It took up operations in 2011.[2] This board is charged with monitoring and analysing financial developments with a view to identifying risks to the financial system. It could also critically accompany

any central bank lending as a last resort to banks and governments. To avoid monetary funding of insolvent governments, central bank lending to governments should only occur through the EMF. The EMF would give financial support to governments cut off from capital markets in return for binding commitments to pursue economic policies aimed at restoring the trust of the markets in their solvency. It would be governed by the finance ministers of EMU member countries, the Eurogroup. In normal times, the EMF would fund its activities in the capital market, issuing bonds backed by its capital and guarantees from its shareholders, the member states of EMU. In times of financial panic, when capital markets seize up, the EMF would have access to ECB funds to carry out its tasks. Credit from the central bank would be given on an application from the EMF, a positive opinion from the ESRB and eventual approval by the ECB's Governing Council.

4. **The EMF supervises national economic policies for consistency with the requirements of monetary union, provides sovereign bond insurance, manages and funds adjustment programmes in case policies do not meet these requirements and manages an orderly debt restructuring of governments and banks in cases of insolvency.** As discussed in previous chapters, flexibility of the economies of member countries – especially in the labour market – and strict fiscal discipline are the prerequisites for the smooth functioning of a common currency area. In the past, surveillance by the European Commission was helpful, but not always effective (e.g., the commission long underestimated the risk emanating from the build-up of current account imbalances among EMU member countries). Hence, like the IMF at the global level, the

EMF would monitor developments in EMU countries so as to ensure that economic developments and policies are consistent with the requirements of EMU. A positive result of the review would qualify a country to have its government bonds insured by the EMF up to the equivalent of 60 per cent of the country's GDP. A negative review would trigger suspension of the insurance of new debt and negotiations of an economic adjustment programme, if necessary coupled with temporary adjustment funding from the EMF. On the launch of a programme funded by the EMF, there would be a standstill on the repayment of outstanding private debt (except interest payments). Debt repayments would resume after the successful conclusion of the programme. In the case of failure of the fiscal-policy part of an adjustment programme, the EMF would arrange a debt restructuring. If the restructuring would create risks to the financial stability of the euro area at large, Brady Plan–type debt swaps (similar to those arranged for Greece in February 2012) could be used to contain the external effects of the debt restructuring. If in addition the programme would fail to restore the balance-of-payments equilibrium of the country, participation of the country in the ECB's interbank payment system would be ended, triggering the country's exit from the euro. The EMF would also provide funds for the restructuring or resolution of insolvent banks and manage the restructuring or resolution in cooperation with the banking authority (EBA, see below).

5. **The ESFS, through its banking, insurance and financial markets agencies, ensures appropriate financial and banking regulation to safeguard financial stability, and through its banking agency provides common deposit**

insurance and manages the restructuring or resolution of insolvent banks. The ESFS with its banking (EBA), insurance (EIOPA) and financial market (ESMA) authorities became operational in 2011. Its purpose is to ensure an EU-wide approach to regulation and supervision. Banks would be required to set aside equity for government debt holdings (which are presently exempted from equity backing, or 'zero-risk-weighted' in the Orwellian language of supervision) and bank exposure to government debt would be treated like exposure to any other single-name debtor (presently government debt is exempt from regulatory ceilings for single-name exposures). With this and the reduction of outstanding government debt, over time the systemic importance of public debtors would decline and eventually end. At the same time, a privately funded euro area–wide deposit insurance scheme (with the EMF as backstop) would eliminate the risk of bank runs caused by concerns over the viability of national guarantee schemes. At present, EU regulation requires deposit insurance for up to EUR 100,000. However, insurance is provided at the national level and hence not credible when a government suffers from a liquidity or solvency crisis. Deposit insurance at the EU level would of course have to go hand in hand with bank restructuring or resolution also at the EU level (or, if this is politically not feasible, at least at the euro area level). To avoid unresolved financial problems from the past leading to transfers from strong to weak banks or countries, banks would have to successfully pass a financial health check before they are allowed to join the common deposit insurance scheme.

A graphical sketch of the proposed new architecture for EMU is given in Chart 11.1.

Chart 11.1. A new architecture for EMU

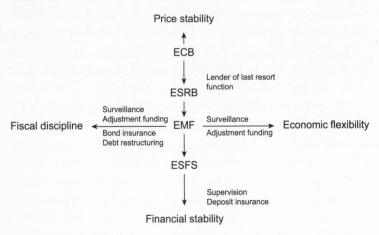

Since the outbreak of the euro crisis in early 2010, we have stumbled towards a new architecture for EMU. At first glance, with the exception of the EMF, the institutions necessary for the above-sketched new architecture for EMU are already in place. Moreover, EU leaders have pledged to strengthen fiscal discipline and improve economic policy coordination among EMU member countries. In principle, the European Stability Mechanism (ESM) could quickly lead to the EMF when the confusion over the role of the ECB as a lender of last resort is resolved. There is nothing in the statutes of the ESM that would prevent it from becoming a counterparty of the ECB and hence gaining access to ECB lending.[3] We have gained experience with adjustment programmes (of a positive nature in the case of Ireland and a negative one in the case of Greece) and with debt restructuring (with Greece as the guinea pig). Last but not least, we are slowly moving towards a European banking regime, which has been dubbed 'banking union'. Hence, it seems that we are firmly on track to rebuild the architecture of EMU in the right way.

Unfortunately, policymakers are still very confused about what a stable architecture of EMU has to look like and may well arrange the building blocks in the wrong way, setting the stage for an eventual break-up of EMU. In my view, the right model for ensuring fiscal discipline in EMU is that of the US in the nineteenth century, where market forces played the most important role. But it seems that key policymakers at the EU level and in Germany are leaning more to the problematic and unstable model of the German Empire, characterized by a weak political control of fiscal policy leading eventually to the monetization of public debt. German chancellor Merkel has insisted that it is necessary to fortify EMU with fiscal or even political union. To this end, she has wanted national sovereignty in key fiscal policy areas transferred from the national to the European level and has held out mutualization of debt as a possible reward. However, as I have explained before, I regard it as very unlikely that the peoples of Europe are willing to cede more sovereignty in key policy areas to European institutions. More likely would be that public debt is mutualized and sovereignty remains national. In that case, EMU would almost certainly break apart as national electorates in stronger countries would refuse to stand in for debt incurred by sovereign decisions in weaker countries. According to EU president Herman van Rompuy, debt restructuring for Greece is supposed to remain 'exceptional and unique', while it should have been held up as an example for the way government insolvency can be treated. Instead of market forces, an intergovernmental treaty is supposed to enforce fiscal discipline of EMU member governments, although experience suggests that such treaties will be broken in times of financial stress. Adjustment funding is kept in place, even when adjustment has failed, as has been the case for Greece. And the ECB is supplying weak banks generously with liquidity so that they can fund their impaired balance sheets and their weak governments. To contemplate the exit of a country from EMU is still difficult in official circles and regarded as politically incorrect when mentioned by critical economists. But it should be clear to all readers who have followed my line of argument so far that this approach to saving EMU will only extend its agony before political disunity over unpaid bills causes its eventual demise.

Because of my relatively pessimistic assessment of the efforts undertaken to rescue EMU, I cannot conclude this book without discussing scenarios for a potential failure of EMU in the remainder of this chapter and in the next. Clearly, the voluntary or forced exit of a smaller country may damage EMU but it would not break it. This is different when a larger country, say Spain or Italy, fails to adjust to the economic and fiscal policy requirements of a common currency area. Given the size of these countries, the funding of government budget and/or current account deficits through the IMF and EFSF/ESM would seem hardly possible.[4] The only source capable of coming up with sufficient funds to replace market funding for these countries would be the ECB. The central bank would continue and expand its relaunched bond purchase programme and its unlimited support for banks in these countries and co-opt them into providing funds for financially troubled governments. Money in search of safe havens, flowing from these countries to the AAA-rated countries, would flood the ECB's interbank payment system with liquidity, eventually creating a level of inflation that electorates there would no longer tolerate. But could these more powerful countries possibly escape from being ensnared in an inflation and transfer union by the weaker countries without creating a major economic, financial and political rupture in Europe?

The printing of money to settle debts inevitably leads to a transfer of real wealth from creditors to debtors. The latter are paid with notes whose power to purchase goods, services or real assets declines. Hence, the inflation created by printing money to stabilize weak governments and banks will inevitably devalue the already outstanding claims of the AAA countries in the form of loans or balance-of-payments credits through the TARGET system. But creditor countries could try to protect themselves against a continued drain of real resources to their weaker partners by pushing up the euro prices for their goods, services and assets so that they are harder to acquire by the debtor countries. To defuse the political and social tensions created by accelerating inflation in the creditor countries themselves, they could temporarily index wages and prices of nominal assets to the rise of their domestic price levels. Thus, higher wages would lead to higher prices for their goods and services, reducing the demand for their products from the debtor countries. Depreciation of the euro against other currencies, caused by the ECB's monetization of government debt and weak bank balance sheets, would maintain competitiveness of the creditor country economies in global markets. In the event, there would be a reduction of exports by creditor countries to debtor countries and an increase of imports of the former from the latter. Creditor country exports to and imports from non–euro area countries would remain stable. Debtor countries would see their total exports rise and their total imports fall. The euro area current account would record a surplus.

Savers in the creditor countries could be protected by inflation-indexed fixed income instruments. For instance, creditor country governments could issue bonds to their residents whose principal and interest payments are linked to the domestic consumer price inflation rate.

Since revenues of these governments would profit from inflation, they would have no problems servicing inflation-indexed debt (as long as this debt does not exceed the share of government revenue in GDP). Governments could also issue inflation-indexed bonds to domestic banks in private placements, allowing these banks to offer inflation-protected savings products backed by these bonds to their customers. To contain fears possibly unleashed by rising inflation, despite the indexation of wages and nominal claims to inflation, governments could offer public assurance and include clauses in their inflation-indexed debt instruments that all indexed financial obligations and claims of the government would be converted into a new currency when domestic euro inflation exceeded a certain level. Private sector participants could calculate the value of the new currency against the euro based on the development of inflation even before the trigger level for a formal switch of currencies is reached. This would allow denominating private contracts in the new currency and establish it initially as a private parallel currency. Savers worried about future weakness of the euro could move their euro assets into the parallel currency, fuelling demand for inflation-linked government debt. Following the formal currency conversion, the new currency would be legal tender only for non-cash transactions with the government and would continue to coexist in all private transactions as parallel currency with the euro, against which its exchange rate would float freely.[5] Thus, all taxes and other government levies would need to be paid in the new currency and the government would settle all payments – including those for wages, government purchases and debt servicing – also in the new currency. Private sector participants would have the choice of making non-cash payments in the new currency or in euros at the prevailing market exchange rate.

In view of the diminishing importance of cash payments and the costs of introducing new cash, the euro would still be accepted for cash payments throughout the monetary union. Such a two-tiered system – one could call it a union within the union – would mimic some elements of the Latin Monetary Union, where common coins coexisted with national paper money. But it would of course differ from the LMU in that only creditor countries would have an incentive to introduce a second-tier currency to protect themselves from the debasing of the euro by debtor countries, and that the exchange rate of the second-tier currency would float – and over time appreciate – against the euro.

Perhaps the creation of such a second-tier currency by the creditor countries may not become necessary after all. The mere option for the creditor countries to do this might be enough to induce the debtor countries to rely less on inflation to devalue their debt and instead strengthen their efforts to fully repay their debt in real terms. Presently, the creditor countries seem to be trapped into a currency that the debtor countries could debase by forcing the central bank to print money so as to prevent default of the debtors and financial collapse. Creditor countries could regain leverage over the debtor countries by developing the option to leave EMU and leave the debtors behind with a debased currency.

Chapter 12

Summary and Conclusions

'I have always found the word 'Europe' on the lips of those who wanted something from others which they dared not demand in their own names!'

—Otto von Bismarck,
German chancellor, in 1880[1]

This book reflects my deliberations on the euro crisis over the last two years, which were stimulated by intense discussions with numerous members of the financial, academic and political communities. Some public comments I made over this period stirred controversy; some of the views I express in this book may still do so. Airing controversial views may be good marketing practice for journalistic or academic commentators (and evidently of book authors). As I found out, going public with such views is a little more difficult for the chief economist of a major European financial institution. Nevertheless, as an economist and convinced European, I felt the need to speak up and live with the consequences.

In narrating my story of the euro I have emphasized the political roots of the single currency of Europe. The origin of EMU must be seen in the context of establishing lasting peace in Europe through ever-closer union among countries which fought two devastating wars against each other in the first half of the last century and were engaged in a cold war with the Soviet Union in the second half. To a considerable extent, the creation of the euro was motivated by the desire to bind a reunified Germany firmly into European political structures so as to control its enhanced economic power. At the same time, however, with the fall of the Berlin Wall and the peaceful unification of Germany, the rationale for European unification as a guarantor for peace in Europe has faded into the background. As another war on European soil has become unthinkable, the goal of a politically united Europe has lost its lustre. Could it be regained by renewing the 'narrative' of the political union, as suggested by some politicians? I do not think so. In view of the insurmountable barriers in language and culture among the various nations of Europe, a full political union of Europe would seem illusionary. In my view, a new 'narrative' for Europe has to focus on the liberties offered by integration: free trade and the free movement of people and capital. But with political union fading into the background, EMU has lost the prospect of a secure platform in the future. It has become necessary to establish EMU as a currency union of sovereign nation states in a unique historical exercise.

Unfortunately, the original architecture of EMU proved to be faulty. Efforts to establish a hard budget constraint for governments through the Stability and Growth Pact have failed; extremely low interest rates and lax credit standards, as well as the treatment of government debt as risk-free in financial regulation and ECB lending practice, have encouraged financial institutions to lend to both private- and public-sector entities lavishly; and a lack of economic discipline has eroded the international competitiveness of a considerable number of EMU member countries. During the first decade of its existence, the cracks in the architecture of EMU were papered over by cheap credit. When the global credit bubble burst, these cracks pushed EMU into crisis. However, the lack of an effective crisis management mechanism led to a piecemeal policy response, which eroded confidence in EMU government and bank debt. Hence, a run on the debt of a number of EMU governments and banks began.

Could the problems have been foreseen and avoided? Perhaps, if mainstream politicians and economists had paid more attention to critical voices such as that of the late Eddie George, governor of the Bank of England, who in the early 1990s had already warned of the pitfalls of a lack of 'real convergence' (of economic growth and labour market developments) and its danger for the stability of a common currency. Recently, a colleague sent me a note I had written in June 2006 and long forgotten. In there, I warned of an 'EMU trap':

> When an EMU member country has lost competitiveness and hence suffers from slowing growth, its government budget deficit tends to widen, leading to an ever greater violation of the Stability and Growth Pact and risk of default on its public debt. The country is now in what we call the EMU trap. We find two countries – Italy and Portugal – presently stuck in the EMU trap, with two more countries – Spain and Greece – rather likely to join them in the not too distant future. In principle, there are three ways to escape the EMU trap. A country can regain competitiveness by deflating production costs; it could leave EMU (at least in theory); or it could use its influence to coax the ECB into tolerating higher inflation at the EMU

level. If our analysis of the nature of the EMU trap is correct, presently complacent investor attitudes – which have compressed bond yield spreads – could suddenly be followed by a high degree of concern. The trigger of such a change in spirits may well be a weakening of growth in Spain and Greece owing to their loss in competitiveness.[2]

By that time, the damage Eddie George had warned of had already been done. But a greater awareness by policymakers of how bad things had become at that time could have brought the development of a crisis management mechanism forward and reduced the economic costs of the euro crisis.

To restore confidence, I have suggested a new architecture for EMU based on five building blocks: (1) EMU governments must be held fully liable for their financial decisions; (2) the central bank must ensure price stability and provide funds of last resort to all systemically important debtors; (3) the central bank acts as lender of last resort in close cooperation with the ESRB and an EMF; (4) the EMF monitors national economic policies, provides adjustment funding to illiquid governments and conducts orderly debt restructurings for insolvent governments and banks; (5) the European System of Financial Supervision ensures an appropriate financial architecture where public-sector debt is considered subject to default risk, manages the restructuring and resolution of insolvent banks in cooperation with the EMF and runs a common deposit insurance scheme. Since not all present and future EMU member countries can be expected to be or remain fit for EMU, exit from EMU without exit from the EU should become possible as a measure of last resort to stabilize the economy.

In 2009, I had already proposed the creation of an EMF and renewed this call together with Daniel Gros of CEPS, the Brussels-based think tank, in early 2010.[3] However, this proposal was met with an icy reception, especially in Germany. Critics warned of the moral hazard created by a bailout of overindebted countries and the dangers of monetary funding of government debt, if the EMF were given access to credits from the ECB. Yet most of the elements in this proposal have been realized over time, albeit in a piecemeal fashion and sometimes not entirely consistently. Access of the EMF to credit from the ECB remains highly controversial at the time I write this. But the denial of central bank funding in a severe liquidity crisis achieves the opposite of what it wants. In the event, the central bank will be dragged into performing the role of lender of last resort, only without legitimacy and hence at the cost of its credibility and reputation.

In contrast to the line pursued by EU officials, I believe that the possibility of sovereign default in EMU is essential to enforce fiscal policy discipline in a monetary union of sovereign states. No set of rules imposed by Brussels can replace the disciplinary influence of the risk of failure. Yes, markets often tend to be complacent, only to suddenly turn with a vengeance against the debtors they so lavishly fed. Therefore, vigilance is required and surveillance of policies by EU institutions is welcome. But sovereign states cannot be ruled from Brussels. The price of sovereignty is liability, and EMU member states have to pay this price if they want to retain sovereignty in key areas of political life. Hence, sovereign default in EMU has to become possible, which requires that its fallout on the financial sector can be managed. Of course, EMU membership is inconsistent with sovereignty in all areas. Members obviously lose sovereignty over monetary policy. But this is not enough.

Monetary policy affects the real economy through the banking system. As we have found, the effectiveness of monetary policy is seriously impaired when banking sector regulation and supervision is left in national hands. Hence, we need to move these tasks to the euro area level, create a 'banking union', as it is now fashionably called. But in doing so we have to strictly observe the principle of subsidiarity: national rule as far as possible, European rule only as far as needed.

Without a new architecture along the lines sketched above, I see the long-term survival of EMU in its present form at risk. But the necessary reforms cannot be implemented against the will of the electorates. Politicians have to seek buy-in from their voters for the sometimes-painful treatment of the ills of EMU. They will not obtain it when EMU is seen as weighing on economic growth and a threat to prosperity. Yes, economic growth is of the essence to reach a stable political base for EMU. But it cannot be generated by government programmes. What are needed are economic policies that instil confidence in companies, private households and foreign lenders. This requires structural reforms to improve international competitiveness, fiscal consolidation (so as to ensure the long-term sustainability of government finances) and the restructuring of the banking sector where needed, to remove the threat of bank failures. All these efforts would benefit from a completion of the Single European Market and financial integration.

Is saving the euro worth the blood, sweat and tears this demands from the members of EMU? Some say no. Some argue that the costs of dissolving EMU are higher than keeping it, so we better get it fixed. This is a very weak defence of the euro. If managed properly in a sound framework, the euro can have tangible benefits for all of its members in the future. Small countries lose sovereignty over their economic policies when large countries experience currency crises and scared investors crowd into safe havens that can harbour few ships. To avoid ruinous currency appreciation caused by panic-driven capital inflows they have to tie their currency – and hence their economic fate – to a large country in crisis. Switzerland can service here as a warning. European countries with national currencies could turn into multiple Switzerlands when the US is haunted by a dollar crisis. As the currency of a large 'country' the euro could offer protection against this. Unfortunately, the odds for a dollar crisis at some time in the future are in my view considerable.

What if we fail to take the necessary medicine to save EMU? Given the need to preserve European political cooperation, mutations of the existing EMU would seem to me more likely than its entire disappearance. I could envisage two potential mutations of EMU in the future. In the first mutation, the ECB would be dragged into monetizing the deficits and debt of insolvent governments. Over time this would lead to the formation of a new, virtual 'hard currency' union within EMU around Germany, with the existing EMU continuing as a 'soft currency' union, along the lines sketched in the previous chapter. As explained there, the hard union could exist within the soft union, with cash shared by all members but the new hard money adopted only by the financially strong members as a second-tier, entirely virtual currency. Apart from the AAA-rated countries – Germany, the Netherlands, Finland and Luxembourg – Austria and a few other Central European EMU member countries with strong government finances might opt for the hard currency. Given the continuing use of euro bills and coins, such a union within the union may just be tolerable politically for France and other Latin

European countries with a preference for a soft currency policy and a higher tolerance of inflation.

In the second mutation, EMU would be reduced to a hard currency union by the exit of all countries unable or unwilling to operate under a hard budget constraint. This could leave a now clearly separate hard currency union with the countries mentioned above and, most likely, France. The latter would be extremely loath to see Germany break all monetary links with itself, given its strong past efforts to bind it into a European monetary union. Of course, French preferences with regard to the conduct of monetary policy would continue to be different from that of Germany and probably most of the smaller remaining members of EMU. Being in the minority in this regard in the small EMU, France would probably feel quite uncomfortable and, as a consequence, press for a strong economic government through which it could protect its economic interests. In this scenario, the countries exiting EMU would be unlikely to find common ground for the creation of another monetary union and probably revert to national currencies. In view of the economic pain for weaker countries of exiting EMU, the first mutation of a hard currency union within a softer EMU would seem more likely than the second one of shrinking EMU to a purely hard currency union.

Past experience is only a very limited guide for the future. Hence, the fact that all monetary unions of sovereign states failed in the past reveals little about the fate of EMU in the future. On the other hand, it would be foolish not to try to learn from the mistakes made in the past. Unfortunately, it seems that not all lessons have already been fully understood. Further efforts are undoubtedly needed to put EMU on a sound and stable base and to have it contribute to the historical work of European unification.

Acknowledgements

This book emerged from countless discussions I had with clients, policymakers and colleagues, and numerous articles and notes I have written since the beginning of the euro crisis (yes, this is more than a mere public debt crisis, as most politicians like to call it) at the end of 2009, after the Greek government owned up to the manipulation of its government finance statistics. Like its main character, the euro, it is unfinished, as the story of the crisis has not yet reached its conclusion. Nevertheless, I felt convinced that the time had come to take stock of where we stand so that we do not entirely lose orientation on the way forward.

As I produced the research on which this book is based, I profited from the cooperation of a number of friends and colleagues. Special thanks go to Daniel Gros for his invaluable advice and his partnership in the development of the concept of a European Monetary Fund. Special thanks also go to Michael Biggs for his innovative concept of the 'credit impulse', to which I had the privilege to contribute. Thanks also go to Hans-Helmut Kotz, Max Watson and several anonymous referees for their valuable comments, and to my colleagues Nicolaus Heinen, Jochen Möbert and Christian Weistroffer for their contributions to research, which I have drawn upon for this book. Aleksandra Klofat and Wladmimir Wogau helped in collecting the material on the history of monetary unions and of the euro. Manjuri Das and Rumki Majumdar provided excellent research assistance. Janka Romero, Rob Reddick and their team went carefully through the manuscript and provided many highly valuable comments. Tej Sood did a great job in managing publication. Of course, all the opinions expressed in this book are my own and should not be assigned to Deutsche Bank, where I was a member of a great research team for many years and with which I am now associated as an advisor. By the same token, all errors are also my own and not of those who so generously gave me help and comments.

Notes

Introduction

1 'Europe will be created through its money or not at all' (in *Revue Synthèses* 45 (1950)).
2 'When the D-Mark does not come to us, we shall come to it!'

Chapter 1   A Question of War and Peace

1 Schuman Plan – declaration of the French government on a common German–French heavy industry, Paris, 9 May 1950.
2 John Maynard Keynes, *The Economic Consequences of the Peace* (Forgotten Books, 1919), 135, quoted in David Marsh, *The Euro* (New Haven: Yale University Press, 2009).
3 Robert Marjolin, *Architect of European Unity: Memoirs 1911–1986* (London: Weidenfeld & Nicolson, 1989), 127.
4 Marjolin, *Memoirs*, 128.
5 Konrad Adenauer, *Erinnerungen 1945–1953* (Stuttgart: Deutsche Verlags-Anstalt, 1965), 312. As Germany did not have a foreign minister at that time, Adenauer used interviews with foreign journalists to send political messages to foreign governments.
6 The theory of economic integration, applied to Europe, distinguishes the following stages (indicated in the textbox): (1) Preferential Trade Agreement; (2) Free Trade Area;

(3) Customs Union (Common External Tariff); (4) Common Market (market freedoms); (5) Economic Union (mutual harmonization); (6) Currency Union; and (7) Political Union.

7 Marjolin, op. cit., 267.

8 See David Graeber, *Debt: The first 5000 years* (New York: Melville House, 2011).

9 See Daniel Gros and Niels Thygesen, *European Monetary Integration* (Harlow: Addison Weasley Longman, 1998), 5.

10 Exchange rate changes went against the objective under the CAP to keep support prices in national currency stable against each other. When exchange rate changes became more frequent, an elaborate system of 'Monetary Compensatory Amounts' was developed to reconcile the 'Green Exchange Rates' under the CAP with actual exchange rates.

11 See David Marsh, *The Euro* (New Haven: Yale University Press, 2009), 45.

12 Gros and Thygesen, op. cit., 12.

13 Proposals to develop the ECU into a common European currency also led nowhere. See Rainer Masera, 'An increasing role for the ECU: A character in search of a script', *Banca d'Italia Temi di Discussione* 65 (1986): 1–62.

14 Gros and Thygesen, op. cit., 177.

15 See Marsh, op. cit., 173.

16 See Anatole Kaletsky, obituary for Richard Medley, *Times* (London), 23 November 2011.

17 See *Bulletin des Presse- und Informationsamts der Bundesregierung* 103/S (26 September 1992): 965.

18 Marsh, op. cit., 181.

Chapter 2   No Longer a Question of War and Peace

1 David Marsh, *The Euro* (New Haven: Yale University Press, 2009), 115.

2 See Daniel Gros and Niels Thygesen, *European Monetary Integration* (Harlow: Addison Weasley Longman, 1998), 396.

3 See ibid., 397.
4 Committee for the Study of Economic and Monetary Union, *Report on economic and monetary union in the European Community* (17 April 1989).
5 Ibid., 15
6 Ibid., 35–6.
7 Marsh, op. cit., 120.
8 Ibid., 121.
9 Ibid., 141.
10 Ibid., 143.
11 Presse- und Informationsamt der Bundesregierung, *Bulletin* 147 (1989): 1243.
12 See Hanns Jürgen Küsters and Daniel Hofmann (eds), *Deutsche Einheit: Sonderedition aus den Akten des Bundeskanzleramts 1989/90* (Munich: R. Oldenbourg, 1998), 638.
13 See 'Wenn Präsidenten lieben', *Die Zeit*, 22 September 2005.
14 Thus, the German magazine *Wirtschaftswoche* quoted high-level officials in Berlin as saying, 'the German-French relations are lousy. They are even worse than at the beginning of Schröder's term.' See Henning Krumrey and Gerhard Bläske, 'Angela Merkels schwieriges Verhältnis zu Nicolas Sarkozy', *Wirtschaftswoche* , 25 May 2010.
15 Otmar Issing, *The Birth of the Euro* (Cambridge: Cambridge University Press, 2008), 12–13.
16 See Presse- und Informationsamt der Bundesregierung, *Bulletin* 103 (26 September 1992): 966.
17 Decisions taken with a qualified majority require a certain number of votes according to keys specified by subject matter but do not require unanimity.
18 Joschka Fischer, 'Vom Staatenverbund zur Föderation – Gedanken über die Finalität der europäischen Integration', speech at Humboldt University, Berlin, 12 May 2000.
19 The 'Monet Method' refers to the process of piecemeal European integration, also called the 'inner logic' of European integration. It was laid out first in the Schuman Plan from May 1950, where the 'making of Europe' was described as a chain of 'concrete facts'.

Chapter 3   A History of Failures

1 http://www.rogerhelmer.com/euroquotes.asp (accessed 7 July 2012).

2 However, the debate over the sharing of the adjustment burden between surplus and deficit countries was not settled once and for all and has continued ever since. When the US ran up large current account deficits in the early 1980s it put pressure on Japan and Germany, which at the time had big surpluses, to boost domestic demand and imports. Since the 1990s, the US has attempted to coax China into action to reduce its current account surplus, and more recently during the euro crisis France has lobbied Germany to boost imports so as to reduce its surplus.

3 See Richard Roberts, 'A stable currency in search of a stable Empire? The Austro-Hungarian experience of monetary union', *History and Policy* (October 2011) and Peter M. Garber and Michael Spencer, 'The Dissolution of the Austro-Hungarian Empire: Lessons for currency reform', *Essays in International Finance* 191 (1994).

4 For a deeper analysis of the problems of the ruble zone see Marek Dabrowski, 'The Reasons of the Collapse of the Ruble Zone', CASE Research Foundation paper (Warsaw, 1995).

5 See also Michael Bordo and Lars Jonung, 'Lessons for EMU from the history of monetary unions', paper presented at IEA Readings, Institute of Economic Affairs, London, 2000.

6 See Carsten Hefeker, 'The agony of central power: Fiscal federalism in the German Reich', *European Review of Economic History* 5 (2001): 119–42.

7 See Niall Ferguson, 'Public Finance and National Security: The Domestic Origins of the First World War Revisited', *Past and Present* 142 (1994): 141–68.

8 See C. Randall Henning and Martin Kessler, 'Fiscal federalism: US history for architects of Europe's fiscal union', paper presented at Bruegel Essays and Lecture Series, 2012.

9 David Graeber, *Debt: The first 5000 years* (New York: Melville House, 2011).

10 Robert A. Mundell, 'A Theory of Optimum Currency Areas', *American Economic Review* 51 (1961): 657–65, and Peter B. Kenen, 'The Theory of Optimum Currency Areas: An Eclectic

View', in Mundell and Swoboda (eds), *Monetary Policy Problems of the International Economy* (Chicago: University of Chicago Press, 1969), 41–60.

11   See 'The future of the euro', report by McKinsey & Company (Germany, January 2012), 13.

12   Ibid., 13.

13   However, as far as the lender of last resort (LORL) function is concerned, Prati and Schinasi note: 'In the area of crisis management, there has been agreement within the Eurosystem on LORL responsibilities. Should a liquidity problem occur, involving an otherwise solvent institution, the provision of emergency liquidity (or LORL) assistance would be the responsibility and decision of the relevant NCB (national central bank). Should this liquidity assistance have an impact on monetary policy, it would entail consultation with the ECB and might also require consultation about whether such liquidity assistance should be provided. In this context, emergency liquidity assistance is defined as liquidity provided to an illiquid, but not insolvent, institution for the purpose of containing systemic risk or contagion, if this is perceived to be a possibility.' See Alessandro Prati and Garry Schinasi, 'Financial Stability in European Economic and Monetary Union', *Princeton Studies in International Finance* 86 (1999): 105. But what if the institution were insolvent and the rescue overtaxed the financial capacity of its home government? What if the government itself was cut off from access to capital markets and faced a liquidity or even solvency crisis? Interestingly, not even Prati and Schinasi raise these questions in their otherwise rather critical report on the arrangements for the maintenance of financial stability in EMU.

Chapter 4   The Euro's Happy Childhood and Its Abrupt End

1   Joaquin Almunia, foreword to 'EMU@10: Successes and challenges after 10 years of Economic and Monetary Union', *European Economy* 2 (2008).

2 http://www.ecb.int/mopo/strategy/pricestab/html/index.
en.html (accessed 7 July 2012).

3 See Michael Biggs and Thomas Mayer, 'Towards a macro-prudential policy framework', *Global Economic Perspectives*, Deutsche Bank, 6 June 2012.

4 See R. Morris, H. Ongena and L. Schuhknecht, 'The reform and implementation of the Stability and Growth Pact', *Occasional Paper Series* 47 (June 2006): 11, 13: 'The SGP that was finally agreed...took the form of EU secondary legislation with decisions to be taken within the standard legislative framework (i.e., Council recommendations or decisions, adopted by qualified majority, on the basis of recommendations by the Commission). The Commission therefore preserved its "right of initiative", while the Council ultimately retained discretion in taking decisions within an overall rules-based framework.'

5 Ibid., 17–18.

6 Ibid., 22.

7 See Almunia, op. cit., 8.

8 In general, current account imbalances were interpreted as a sign of financial integration made possible by the elimination of exchange rate risk: 'National economic policies have become better coordinated, and in the case of monetary policy it has even been completely merged. A relevant factor for some euro area member countries is that the risk of possible speculative attacks on national currencies has been removed. Not so long ago, in the pre-EMU past, the impact of movements by the Deutsche Mark against the US dollar was often aggravated by similar movements against euro legacy currencies: this can no longer happen. Clearly, there are also general economic benefits arising from more financial integration in the euro area. I will mention a few here. Financial integration fosters financial development, the modernization of the financial system and, ultimately, economic growth... Thanks to greater financial integration, economic agents can invest more easily in any part of the euro area and thereby spread the risk of potential local shocks having an impact on income and consumption. The potential

NOTES

227

benefits of this are very significant. As euro area investors assign more weight to portfolio investment in euro area countries – and banking integration grows as well – risk-sharing in the euro area increases. This is a very important shock absorber.' Speech by Jean-Claude Trichet, president of the ECB, at the 57. Jahresversammlung des Ifo Instituts für Wirtschaftsforschung an der Universität München, Munich, 29 June 2006.

9 Jean-Claude Trichet, ECB press conference, Frankfurt, 6 March 2008.

Chapter 5   A Crisis of Legitimacy

1 Horst Köhler, interview in *Der Spiegel*, 6 April 1992.
2 Banks were even persuaded by officials to raise their government bond holdings when other investors withdrew. They could finance their bond purchases by using the acquired bonds as collateral for borrowing from the ECB. When the rating of Greece fell below the limit for eligible collateral, the ECB waived the limit for Greece.
3 The notion that there should be something like a 'national banking system' within EMU is a fallacy. In a currency union, banks should operate across regions with a view to diversifying both investment and funding risk. However, a true euro area banking sector has not emerged so far. Hence, banks in individual countries have remained heavily exposed to country-specific risk with the result that a sovereign debt problem in an EMU member country directly leads to a banking problem in this country.
4 Perhaps the most famous proposal in this regard originated from Jacques Delpla, a French economist and government adviser, and was subsequently developed by the Brussels-based Bruegel Institute. See Jakob von Weizsäcker and Jacques Delpla, 'Eurobonds: The blue bond concept and its implications' Bruegel Policy Contribution 2011/02 (21 March 2011).
5 See European Commission, 'Feasibility of Introducing Stability Bonds', green paper (Brussels, 2011).

Chapter 6   A (Hidden) Balance-of-Payments Crisis

1 European Central Bank, *Monthly Bulletin* (November 2011): 35–6.
2 Ibid, 35.
3 See Hans-Werner Sinn and Timo Wollmershaeuser, 'Target Loans, Current Account Balances and Capital Flows: The ECB's Rescue Facility', CESifo Working Paper 3500 (2011).
4 ECB, op. cit., 39.

Chapter 7   Forward or Backward?

1 Jens Weidmann, 'The crisis as a challenge for the euro area', speech at the Association of Family Enterprises, Cologne, 13 September 2011.
2 See 'Quotes about the EU, the euro and Europe', http://www.teameurope.info/node/19 (accessed 30 June 2012).
3 Bundesbank, *Annual Report* (Frankfurt, 1995).
4 Jean-Claude Trichet, 'Building Europe, building institutions', speech on receiving the Karlspries 2011, Aachen, 2 June 2011.
5 See US Department of State, 'Background Note: Greece 12/09/11', http://www.state.gov/outofdate/bgn/greece/186730.htm (accessed 30 June 2012).
6 Michalis Chrysochoidis, interview in *Frankfurt Allgemeine Zeitung*, 9 February 2012.
7 Martin Schulz, interview in *Frankfurter Allgemeine Zeitung*, 13 April 2012, 4.
8 See EFSF, 'Frequently Asked Questions', http://www.efsf.europa.eu/attachments/faq_en.pdf (accessed 30 June 2012).
9 See Jakob von Weizsäcker and Jacques Delpla, 'The Blue Bond Proposal', Bruegel Policy Brief (6 May 2010) and Hans-Joachim Dübel, 'Partial sovereign bond insurance by the euro zone: A more efficient alternative to blue (Euro) bonds', CEPS Policy Brief 252 (August 2011).

229

10 I suggested such an institution already in 2009 and renewed the proposal in early 2010 against the background of the emerging crisis in Greece. See Thomas Mayer, 'The Case for a European Monetary Fund', *Intereconomics* 3 (May/June 2009) and Daniel Gros and Thomas Mayer, 'How to deal with sovereign default: Towards a Euro(pean) Monetary Fund', CEPS Policy Brief 202 (February 2010).

11 ESM statutes: Treaty Establishing the European Stability Mechanism, doc T/ESM 2012/en 10.

Chapter 8   In Search of a Lender of Last Resort

1 Otmar Issing, 'Moral hazard will result from ECB bond buying', *Financial Times*, 1 December 2011.

2 See Liaquat Ahamed, *Lords of Finance: The Bankers Who Broke the World* (New York: Penguin Press, 2009), for a vivid description of both historic events.

3 Issing, op. cit.

4 Daniel Gros and Thomas Mayer, 'Refinancing the EFSF via the ECB' (revised version), *CEPS Commentary*, 18 August 2011.

Chapter 9   The Politics of Euro Rescue

1 Speech on 26 October 2011 in the Bundestag.

2 McKinsey & Company, 'The future of the euro: An economic perspective on the euro crisis', report (January 2012).

3 These savings were already identified in a study by the European Commission in 1990. See 'One market, one money. An evaluation of the potential benefits and costs of forming an economic and monetary union', *European Economy* 44 (October 1990).

4 McKinsey & Company, op. cit., 11.

5 Helmut Kohl, 'Wir muessen wieder Zuversicht geben', interview in *Internationale Politik*, May 2011.

6 Uncertain whether enough investors would 'voluntarily' participate in the debt swap, the Greek authorities introduced retroactively collective action clauses into bonds issued under Greek law (more than 90 per cent of all outstanding Greek government bonds). The ECB obtained bonds with new serial numbers so as to make sure that they would not have to participate in the debt swap when holders of a certain bond had decided with a qualified majority (66 per cent with a participation in the vote of at least 50 per cent of bond holders) to engage in the debt exchange.

7 See Thomas Mayer, 'The Geuro: A parallel currency for Greece?' *Global Economic Perspectives*, Deutsche Bank, 18 May 2012.

8 See interview in *Frankfurter Allgemeine Zeitung*, 13 April 2012, 4.

Chapter 10   Why Europe Needs the Euro

1 Thilo Sarrazin, *Europa braucht den Euro nicht* (Munich: Deutsche Verlagsanstalt, 2012).

2 The examples of UK and Sweden, where the effects of monetary policy spillover from larger countries has not been an issue, do not contradict my point. Where inflation and monetary policy preferences between small and large countries are aligned, conflicts over the exchange rate do not arise.

3 In his memoirs, Alan Greenspan recalls, 'Early in 1980, letters from people who'd been put out of work flooded Volcker's office' and says that 'doing what Volcker did took exceptional courage'. Alan Greenspan, *The Age of Turbulence* (New York and London: Penguin, 2007) 85–6.

4 An alternative view is that of the Post-Keynesian school associated with the late Hyman Minsky. There, economic agents do not always behave rationally but are driven by 'animal spirits'. These make them prone to follow speculative waves, which create financial bubbles. To avoid this, the Post-Keynesians not only favour constructivist macroeconomic

policies but also strict regulations in the financial sector. What is the source of the problem for the Austrians – constructivist economic policies – is the solution for the Post-Keynesians. The problem is that Keynesian policies were widely tested in the 1970s and failed.

5 Edward Shaw and Ronald McKinnon coined this term in 1973 for financial conditions in emerging market economies. See Edward S. Shaw, *Financial Deepening in Economic Development* (New York: Oxford University Press, 1973) and Ronald I. McKinnon, *Money and Capital in Economic Development* (Washington DC: Brookings Institute, 1973).

6 Recently, Carmen Reinhart and Belen Sbrancia have revived the term to describe the likely exit from public overindebtedness. See Carmen M. Reinhart and M. Belen Sbrancia, 'The Liquidation of Government Debt', NBER Working Paper 16893 (March 2011).

Chapter 11   A New Foundation for EMU

1 'We are trapped', *Frankfurter Allgemeine Zeitung*, 18 February 2012, 12.

2 For a review of the new arrangements for financial supervision in the EU, see Bernhard Speyer, 'Financial Supervision in the EU', Deutsche Bank Research *EU Monitor* 84 (4 August 2011).

3 For a discussion of the economic and legal aspects of turning the ESM into a bank – and hence effectively into an EMF – see Daniel Gros and Thomas Mayer, 'Liquidity in times of crisis: Even the ESM needs it', CEPS Policy Brief 265 (March 2012).

4 Moreover, given the seniority of the IMF and ESM, the greater the financial support from these institutions becomes, the more difficult it is for countries to return as borrowers to private markets, because investors demand an additional risk premium for having to bear the first loss in case of default. Hence, should the architecture of EMU be overhauled again, lending by the ESM (or better the proposed EMF) should

become *pari passu* with private sector lending (as has been case for the EFSF).

5 There have been numerous proposals for introducing a common European currency as a parallel currency. Notably, in November 1989, the UK government proposed such a scheme as an alternative to the Delors Plan. In principle, a parallel currency could also be introduced by the private sector on its own. It could quickly gain acceptance as a means of payment and store of value if banks back it with gold holdings. When issuance of the private parallel currency has reached a critical mass, the public sector may get involved by creating a central bank to serve as a lender of last resort of the gold-backed currency to commercial banks.

Chapter 12   Summary and Conclusions

1 TEAM, 'Quotes about the EU, the euro and Europe', http://www.teameurope.info/node/19 (accessed 30 June 2012).
2 See Deutsche Bank, 'Beware of the EMU Trap', *Focus Europe*, 19 June 2006.
3 See Thomas Mayer, 'The Case for a European Monetary Fund', *Intereconomics* 3 (May/June 2009) and Daniel Gros and Thomas Mayer, 'How to deal with sovereign default: Towards a Euro(pean) Monetary Fund', CEPS Policy Brief 202 (February 2010).

Index

Numbers in bold indicate information found in charts, tables or textboxes